775

Walker-Ames Lectures

LITERARY STUDY

And

The Scholarly Profession

By HARDIN CRAIG

Essay Index Reprint Series

BOOKS FOR LIBRARIES PRESS

FREEPORT, NEW YORK

STANDARD BOOK NUMBER:

8369-1079-6

LIBRARY OF CONGRESS CATALOG CARD NUMBER:

72-84303

PRINTED IN THE UNITED STATES OF AMERICA

FOREWORD

By the will of Maude Walker Ames, "The Walker-Ames Fund of the University of Washington" was established in 1931 "to perpetuate the names and memory of William Walker and Emma Williams Walker, his wife, Maude Walker Ames, their daughter, and E. G. Ames, her husband."

Among other stipulations for the use of this bequest, Mrs. Ames stated that "the income of the Walker-Ames Fund may be used for the establishment and maintenance of special lectureships or visiting professorships to which distinguished scientists, artists, writers, teachers, thinkers, men of affairs, and other distinguished persons not in the service of the University of Washington may be called to the University of Washington for such periods of service in teaching or research as the Board of Regents may determine. The income from said fund may be used as needed not only for the honorarium or salary which may attach to such service, but also for such incidental expenses as may attach to the effective use of such special lecturers or visiting professors, such as special books, materials and equipment, publication of lectures, and other outlays needed for the effectiveness of their work."

In accordance with the terms of the will, the University has, since 1931, engaged the services of outstanding scholars in various fields for short periods. Quite generally, in addition to his more technical work with students, the visitor has delivered a series of lectures to the public and thus the community as a whole has shared in the good fortune of the University.

This publication of the Walker-Ames Fund seeks to give permanence to the ten public lectures delivered by Professor Hardin Craig during the spring of 1944 while he was Walker-Ames Professor at the University of Washington. The timely emphasis on scholarly ideals and professional standards makes the book particularly useful to teachers, research men, and advanced students, but there is much in it which will help the non-professional person to a better understanding of the problems which beset the scholar.

Professor Craig is a Shakespearean specialist, with a lively interest in the relation of literature to the philosophical, social, and scientific backgrounds of an educated society. He received his B.A. from Centre College and his M.A. and Ph.D. degrees from Princeton University; the honorary degree, Dottore dell' Università di Pádova, was conferred in 1922; and periods of research were spent at Exeter College, Oxford, the British Museum, and the Huntington Library, where he was Research Associate. He has taught at Princeton, University of Minnesota, University of Chicago, State University of Iowa, and Stanford University, and is now a member of the faculty of the University of North Carolina.

Renaissance Studies in Honor of Hardin Craig, a complimentary volume of scholarly essays published jointly by Stanford University and the University of Iowa, includes an interesting biographical sketch, as well as a full bibliography of Professor Craig's published writings. Among these are *Recent Literature of the English Renaissance*, a bibliography published each year since 1925, many significant articles on medieval drama, editions of Shakespeare, Machiavelli's *Prince*, Byron, Metham, Swift, Poe, and English novelists. Now in press are a complete edition of *Shakespeare's Works*, a history of English literature (in collaboration with Anderson, Bredvold, and Beach), and the Stockton Axson Memorial lectures delivered at Rice Institute in 1943.

The University of Washington is pleased to be able to offer to the general public the work of such an eminent scholar.

D. D. GRIFFITH,
Department of English

PREFACE

I wish, first of all, to acknowledge the honor done me by the University of Washington in appointing me Walker-Ames Professor for the spring term of the year, 1944. I am particularly grateful for the opportunity to gather together in the form of lectures a good deal of what I have learned from my experience as a teacher of English literature in a number of different American universities. I should probably never have done it but for the opportunity, I may say also the compulsion, of doing it systematically and in such form as to be intelligible to an academic community. I am still not sure it was worth doing, and can only say that, after many years as a professor in classrooms, on committees, and faculties, it was a pleasure to do it. I have tried to be very honest in the record of my own opinions, although I realize that these opinions are, for the most part, not startling or of profound originality.

I realize also that I have not talked about literature as much as I had expected to do, although my intention from the start was to discuss, not literature as such, but literature as a study, and, further, literature as a study in American colleges and universities. Even so, the interconnections of literature with other branches of study is such that one has to consider the whole field of study along with literature. University regulations, trends of preference, the lives students live and the ideals they adopt—all these and other factors determine what literature and other humanistic studies may hope to accomplish, so that it may seem that I have really written a book on American higher education. In any case, the book has no pretense to importance in what it says about literature. The subject is what Bacon would have described as "sufficiently laboured or undertaken." This book deals with literature as a subject of study and sometimes of research in American institutions of learning, and not with the far more important subject of the nature and function of literature in society. It deals with personal opinions, not unquestionable truths to be imparted with the authority of superior insight, and its merit, if it has one, is in its frankness. Possibly, as a record or result of sincere interest and no small amount of effort, it may commend itself to readers who have the same love of literature that I have and something of my faith in the educational value of poetry, drama, and fiction.

To read *The Scholemaster* and translate it into terms of application to modern education is an almost uncanny experience. One begins to suspect that Ascham, when he wrote that book, had been lurking around Stanford, Princeton, the State University of Iowa, or some other American university. Some students would know that such a thing is chronologically impossible, a few would suspect that it is not chronologically impossible, and the rest would say, "It's all right by me." The "Circe's court" of Italy we have not only renamed Hollywood or Broadway, but have by movies and various other means moved it to our own campuses. We seem to have all the ills of which Ascham complained, and in addition to them all that have come from commercialism and coeducation. We have also "marvelous" cases of young gentlemen who are "ashamed of good learning, and never a whit ashamed of ill manners." We have those who dispraise learning and say that "without learning, common experience, knowledge of all fashions, and haunting all companies shall work in youth both wisdom and ability to execute any weighty affair," in spite of the plain statement of Erasmus that "experience is the common schoolhouse of fools." It seems also that in those days college men dressed flashily and behaved in public in such a way as to establish false ideals in the minds of poor boys in the community.

The revelations made by Bacon in *The Advancement of Learning* are even more disastrous than those of Ascham. Bacon was no prophet by profession, so it must be that all men who ascertain and speak the exact truth are of necessity prophets. I do not follow up this idea for fear of uttering heresy, but it is true that prophecy and honest, current truth have a most significant way of falling together. To remind the reader of the things that Bacon said about the learning and the institutions of learning in his day which still apply to learning and institutions of learning in our day, I should have to repeat large sections of *The Advancement of Learning*. He did say, "Among so many great foundations of colleges in Europe, I find it strange that they are all dedicated to professions, and none left free to arts and sciences at large." He goes on to remark that, although "it is necessary to the progression of science that readers be of the most able and sufficient men," there is discoverable a great defect, "namely, in the smallness and meanness of the salary or reward which in most places is assigned unto them." And he also declares that men are prone to "sell their books and to build furnaces; quitting and forsaking Minerva and the Muses as barren virgins, and relying upon Vulcan." He also admits that "visitation," by which I take it he means administrative supervision, is rather ignorant of what it is "visiting."

Bacon's diagnosis of the "distempers or diseases" of learning of his day is well known, and I wish we could feel assured that our learning is entirely cured of these distempers or even in the way of intelligent treatment. We still seem to study words and not matter, of which words "are but the images." We still have "an unprofitable subtlety" both as to subject and as to manner or method. We no longer go in for disputations, but we do break up the solidity of sciences with minutiae—*Quaestionum minutiis scientiarum frangunt soliditatem.* Our favorite way of doing this is by giving college credit for matters of play and amusement. And, finally, we cannot say that we are free from "the third vice or disease of learning, which concerneth deceit or untruth, . . . for the truth of being and the truth of knowing are one, differing no more than the direct beam and the beam reflected. This vice therefore brancheth itself into two sorts: delight in deceiving, and aptness to be deceived; imposture and credulity."

So it looks, all in all, as if we had not made much gain in higher education since the days of Roger Ascham and Francis Bacon. To be sure, we have done pretty well in brick and stone, but I call those sixteenth-century buildings at Oxford and Cambridge to witness that we have not done any better than Ascham's and Bacon's ages did. No honest man can say that we have realized Bacon's ideal, and my great fear is that such a person might say that we have almost lost sight of it:

But the greatest error of all the rest [Bacon says] is the mistaking or misplacing of the last or furthest end of knowledge. For men have entered into a desire of learning and knowledge, sometimes upon a natural curiosity and inquisitive appetite; sometimes to entertain their minds with variety and delight; sometimes for ornament and reputation; and sometimes to enable them to victory of wit and contradiction; and most times for lucre and profession; and seldom sincerely to give a true account of their gift of reason, to the benefit and use of men: as if there were sought in knowledge a couch whereupon to rest a searching and restless spirit; or a terrace for a wandering and variable mind to walk up and down with a fair prospect; or a tower of state for a proud mind to raise itself upon; or a fort or commanding ground for strife and contention; or a shop for profit or sale; and not a rich storehouse for the glory of the Creator and the relief of man's estate.

We shall not arrive in my day or in that of any living man at the truth, the whole truth, and nothing but the truth about the actual situation, the function, or the correct procedures of higher education in our country; but, as Churchill remarked about winning the war in the air, there is no harm in trying. Of course, truth, as thought of here, is relative to the institution, the times, and the aims of education, and they, too, are relative to our society; so, perhaps, I am too conscious of the power of the enemies of education and of our own inadequacy. Such a thing would be understandable in a man of my age. But I have at least pointed out, as clearly as possible, what seemed to me the chief dangers in our present higher education. I have thought that the home, the church, and the school are all giving ground before a wave of thoughtless social, commercial, and material diversion, and that institutions of higher learning themselves are suffering defeat. I hope, if I am right about it, that these disruptive forces will exhaust themselves, like a hurricane at sea, and that our country will have the merit to right itself after the storm abates. We have always prided ourselves in America on our ability to absorb and assimilate all sorts of indigestible things, and the very head and front of my offending hath this extent, no more, that I think, in the first place, that we have a lot of assimilating yet to do; and, in the second, I have presumed to say that I think we who are responsible for American higher education ought to do something about it; that we actually ought to go to work at our jobs with renewed and purposeful vigor. There are a lot of things we can do if we only have the industry and the courage to try.

If it is objected that a mere teacher of English literature is not called upon to concern himself with matters that pertain to the whole range of education, I can only humbly say with Sidney "that self-love is better than any gilding to make that gorgeous wherein ourselves be parties."

I have been reading a good many books and articles on current aspects of American education, and have tried to give credit at the appropriate places in the lectures for words and ideas which have been taken from others. I have an uneasy feeling that there may be small bits here and there which have not been attributed to their original authors. If this is true, I am very sorry; but perhaps I may be forgiven on the grounds that, having been a generous teacher for many years, I might be allowed on this occasion to snap up a few unconsidered trifles on my own account.

The quotations which have been placed before the lectures are from Bishop Butler, most of them from his *Analogy*, a book read with some labor and pain when I was at Centre College many years ago.

CONTENTS

CHAPTER I

THE FIELD OF ACTION AND ENDEAVOR

But the practical question in all cases is, whether the evidence for a course of action be such, as, taking in all circumstances, makes the faculty within us, which is the guide and judge of conduct, determine that course of action to be prudent. Indeed, satisfaction that it will be for our interest or happiness, abundantly determines an action to be prudent: but evidence almost infinitely lower than this determines actions to be so too; even in the conduct of every day.

B Y "LITERARY STUDY" in the title of this course of lectures is meant quite definitely literature as an academic discipline. The lectures are a reflection of long experience in the study and teaching of English literature in American universities and colleges and do not pretend to solve philosophic questions as to the nature of literature and art or to present a consistent idea of the function of literature in society at large. My intention is much more humble. I intend to study what we are doing and how we are doing it, and even here it is only certain aspects of the study of literature that come up for consideration. There will be, for example, no study of principles of curriculum-making, no particular consideration of language, literature, and composition as the three main fields of our activity in colleges, and no attempt to guide or to dictate matters of choice within the field of literature or among courses and points of view. I do not think I can solve all the problems of humanistic education, and I do not intend to try.

There are many ways of studying literature, many points of view. They are, as far as I know, all justifiable and most of them desirable. I merely record and explain the aims and problems of my own work as scholar and teacher during the last forty years and more. There are two principal ways, two main aspects of literature as studied in American institutions of higher learning: literature as an art and literature as a branch of human history; and, although my own activities as a scholar have been mainly in the latter field, I have, I think, been always keenly aware of the charm and power of literature as an art. I disclaim any belief that my way is the best way, much less that it is the only proper way, to study literature. So far as the practice of the art of literature is concerned, I have always regarded creative activity with hope and with an admiration just short of envy.

You will find me in this course of lectures talking as a scholar and, up to the limit of my ability, as a man of learning, and also giving expression to the values which have appealed to me as I employed literature as a means of improving the culture of my pupils at a number of places widely scattered throughout our country. There is, perhaps, in all this an acceptance of things as they are or as they might become, an acceptance based on the belief that there is no one and only correct way to study literature and employ it as a tool in the education of the young. I base my opinions on a concept of the unity and independence of the individual and on the similarity of individuals. This concept will be our first concern. It is not, accordingly, a question of whether or not teachers of literature write poetry and fiction, whether or not they seek to occupy a critical attitude and endeavor to teach to their pupils a critical rather than an historical attitude, or whether or not they write and publish any books and articles or operate exclusively as teachers and expositors of literature. It is rather a question of what we are able to do and to be in whatever line of activity we choose to follow. The question is, can we by the grace of God be or become something satisfactory to our best selves and useful to our fellow men? The answer does not lie altogether with our wills, for we are conditioned by the brains we have, the bodies we have, and alas! in organized society by the opportunities we are able to select or have thrust upon us or have denied us altogether. I cannot believe that there is any hopeless breach between scholarship and literary interpretation or between research scholarship and teaching, that is, if these things are truly what they profess to be. I see nothing in the nature of their practice which within reasonable limits makes them mutually exclusive forms of academic exercise.

In approaching the nature and operation of research into truth let me first bring to your attention the familiar steps followed in ascertaining what we think of as truth, from which we arrive at a sort of satisfaction or reassurance with reference to the knowledge of our environment. The contest between man and his environment may be described as life, experience, and knowledge, and the following are the formal steps which we take in finding out truth or probability with reference to our environment.

First, we perceive the existence of a problem. We have a desire to fulfill, a choice to make, a danger to avoid, or a curiosity to satisfy. Our urge may range from the coolest objectivity to the direst personal emergency. There is something before us which has a reference to the immediate or the remote future, something usually which must be ascertained as a pattern of action or of avoidance.

The next stage is an examination of particulars as complete as circumstances, our will, and our ability permit it to be. This is an analytical process and is the normal and practical measure of character and intellect.

The third step is the classification of particulars with reference to classes already known or apprehended or hitherto unknown. It may be so nearly a mere flash that we are unconscious of it. It may, on the other hand, be an enduring puzzle or a despairing bewilderment. This process is partly analytic and partly synthetic.

In the fourth stage we usually arrive at what seems to be a solution of our question. In the light of all the facts at our command we decide upon such and such an explanation of our problem. This is called in science an hypothesis. It may have to us a maximum degree of probability, but no complete certainty. I speak of ordinary cases and am myself rather puzzled by the quality ascribed to Newton according to which even the complicated problems of Euclid seemed axiomatic and not in need of any proof.

The fifth step is an operation the purpose of which is to pass over from the realm of probability to the realm of proof. It is called verification. The possibility of this step depends on whether or not the material is of such a nature that it can be manipulated, bound and compelled, checked and hedged in, to such a degree that phenomena can be made to repeat themselves at the will of the experimenter. In this way the solution proposed may be, as we say, verified or its falsity made evident. Bacon first saw the possibility of this procedure, also its necessity for scientific progress. It is perhaps his greatest gift to posterity. The process of verification thus depends on the possibility of controlling the environment, so that certain operating factors may be identified.

From the possibility or impossibility of the operation arises the division between the natural, or let us say the laboratory, sciences, on the one hand, and the social sciences and what we call the humanities, on the other. Many subjects of the greatest importance cannot be so controlled, and for them probability is the uttermost goal which may be reached. Let me again remind you of the mind of Newton and ask you to speculate with me on the possibility of intuitional certainty and even of revealed truth.

In any case we need not disturb ourselves with the thought that probability is, in most of our endeavor, our extreme limit. Bishop Butler saw that the vast body of the procedures of human life rests on probability alone. As he put it, "Probability is the very guide of life." A knowledge of the relation of the "proof" subjects, such as physics, chemistry, and the biological sciences, to the "probability" subjects, such as anthropology, history, economics, jurisprudence, government, and for the most part psychology, will enable us to assess correctly the claims of both groups and will enable us to know where we are going when we leave the realm of science altogether and enter the field of the humanities.

It is obvious that the natural scientists, and let us say also the mathematicians, have a great advantage in the nature of their fields and in the fact that their errors are quickly apparent, as also in the readiness with which their discoveries can be adopted, applied, and made to yield results, often material rewards; but they are not the only searchers after truth, and their discoveries are not the only ones of importance in the world. Their discoveries have only their own proper value and, beyond this value, it is never claimed that they are adequate. Witness the maladjustment of the society and politics of the world in the very time of man's greatest advancement in the laboratory sciences. The advancement of science is not responsible for this war, but scientific discoveries have added to its destructiveness and its horrors. The war has arisen, not from the advancement of the laboratory sciences, but from the relative backwardness of the social sciences, and still more from the greed, the gullibility, and the hardness of the human heart. The human heart sits squarely in the middle of the relatively obscure terrain of the humanities. In the humanistic fields men have not determined where our greatest happiness lies and have not agreed upon or have forgotten what truth is. It is an appalling thought that they may never learn and never agree.

I draw only one rough distinction and do not pretend to offer a classification of the fields of learning. I believe that the distinction I make is valid and useful, and, in order to understand its application to various kinds of human knowledge, I should like to draw a sort of map of man's environment and his relation to it, an analysis which I owe to Professor Myron F. Brightfield of the University of California. Each man exists for an interval of time within "a set of spatially manifest surroundings." This, his environment, recognizes no responsibility for him. In order to exist he must directly or vicariously sustain his life. He needs food, shelter, and the satisfaction of certain biological and social instincts. In this environment some things are favorable, some neutral, some hostile. Whether he likes it or not, man must enter into a struggle with his environment, must assume the rôle of an aggressor, for even to refuse the contest is to enter it. The fight is usually at the barriers or in the enemies' territory, so that man appears to fight against odds, or, as we say, to pass through a vale of tears. But there are certain things he can and does do. He can observe, choose, reject, measure, and estimate. He can advance or retard, destroy or foster, rebel against or acquiesce in natural changes. He has memory to record and judgment to compare experiences. He can make plans, use tools, and store up advantages in the form of wealth and beneficial position. He has, in addition, a social environment and varied personal traits of which he may take advantage or which may destroy him. My position with reference to man's freedom is pragmatical or traditionary, as you may choose to consider it.

We may present this total environment as a series of three concentric groups. Man is at the center. The innermost group is the self, the family, and the neighborhood. Its test is face-to-face association, its quality is uniqueness; but it is not isolated or independent. The next of these concentric groups is that made up of larger numbers of people. It includes vocation, religion, social classification, politics, nationality, sports, clubs, language, and race. The third and outermost ring includes such universal characteristics of man as heredity, sex, certain matters pertaining to race, and human nature itself. There is no choice in membership in this circle, which comes from being alive in the world. A certain part of this outermost circle of man's environment constitutes the field of the experimental sciences. Other parts are beyond the scope of their manipulations.

I pause long enough to remind you that actually the fields are not segregated spatially. Each unit is in the whole field and cannot be withdrawn into any portion of it. It follows that no aspect is discrete or separable (except in abstraction) from any other aspect. The individual man is always in the whole field or at least is so placed that he may at any moment be impressed by any object within the whole field. We can look here and there, but we can neither see nor escape the whole. This speculation, which suggests the fourth dimension, may at any rate be suggestive of a synthetical as distinguished from an analytical approach to the problem of man's relation to his environment.

These features of the environment are united by many elements, whose interplay is infinitely varied. Marriage is the typical illustration of this complexity. It draws its impulse from sex; it is surrounded with the regulations of the second circle and is the main formative element in the innermost circle in which man lives. It must also be remembered that even the innermost circle is not controlling in its operation and that the individual is the center of reference. The innermost circle is small in quantity relative to the others; it has little plan or purpose; and is, relatively speaking, temporary in duration and casual in character. It is therefore little subject to scientific study except as it is influenced by forces from the outside, mainly from the second circle.

The second circle itself is the battleground of life and learning. Its groups are large. Its principles of cohesion are strong and they are conflicting and doubtful or unknown. Its features are capable of being organized according to purpose and function, and they have, many of them, enduring status. Government, language, economics, religion, morals, vocations, recreational activity, war, peace, sectionalism, propaganda, fashion, and many other things are the *terra incognita* of experimental science. We call it the field of social science. Its claims to consideration are hortatory, and it relies for its determination of truth on probability; little or no absolute proof is possible, and in the way of acceptance lie many obstacles. Its memberships are partly voluntary. It has benefits to confer and inherited rights to maintain, or rights acquired. As the rights of one class impinge on another or hinder the desires of individuals, we have causes for contest and need of truth.

It is not so much that we do not know what things are or what the consequences will be as the fact that we cannot get the truth accepted, for every sort of conservatism of mind and habit blocks the way, and false ideas stand forth and continually claim to be accepted as truth. The commoner errors were described by Bacon in his famous description of the Idols in *Novum Organum*. The determination of dependable standards in many of the fields is not impossible. We at least know that time exerts influence on the social environment. The individual, though set in the flow of temporal circumstance, has possible choices to make on which depends in some measure his happiness. Ultimately he will succumb to poverty, illness, or old age, but we think his fall may be mitigated. Again in the middle area time operates, but more slowly. It is hardly felt in the outermost circle. The outermost circle is stable, the innermost circle has little or no stability, the middle circle has a certain stability. Generality stands at one end and uniqueness at the other.

Human experience and knowledge are made highly complex by the circumstances of environment and by the influence of time. Man strives for a margin of survival above the food for the day, the house for the night, and the desires for propagation of species. He gains possessions and with them security. With this security enter also plans for the future of himself and his household. It will clarify this matter sufficiently if I say that man is not independent and that he needs to discover truth and explore it. All men need it for their health if for nothing else. Many men need it because ignorance and error destroy their happiness. No man is independent. And almost no man is without a measure of prudence by which he seeks to guide his life.

We have thus a seeker after truth or man engaged or willing to engage in research. Secondly, a subject-matter; thirdly, a system of classification within the field; fourthly, a method of procedure. We can illustrate this list of essentials from the mind of the eighteenth century. It had an impulse to learn. It had set its political house somewhat in order, for it had discovered that it wanted no absolute kings or kings of the Catholic faith. Locke had seen that the older psychology was erroneous and untrue to the nature of the human mind. He had also seen that credit and not coin is the basis of commerce. Many other discoveries and adjustments had been made. Shaftesbury put forward hypotheses to the effect that man is a part of nature. Johnson saw that there was need of a sounder dictionary, Burke that government was a matter of consent of the governed and also a manifestation of principles of social justice. Pope was convinced that Bolingbroke and Shaftesbury were right in their hypothesis about man and nature and made of himself a most excellent propagandist. Berkeley developed the philosophy of idealism, Hume the philosophy of criticism. And so on. All these men were engaged in putting forward as probable certain hypotheses. They did not gain immediate acceptance for the most part, but by putting forward and determining the limits and bearings of their ideas they brought them before their generation and later generations, so that their ideas might be known and, as we say, tested by experience. It may be said that the eighteenth century discovered the utility of the probable. Bishop Joseph Butler explained the theory.

Because of the devastating effect of fallacy or error on the progress of human culture, particularly in the field of the humanities, I wish to embody in this lecture a statement of the nature of argument and the establishment of probability. Testimony and authority are and will always be greatly used in any field to which they apply. They are indispensable for the conservation of such truths as society has ascertained. The Bible has been of inestimable value because of its tested wisdom. So have Aristotle, Plato, and the classics. But in those matters thrown up by the stream of time for which there is no reliable precedent, testimony and authority are of small value except as they may have generated a habit of testing and other habits such as conservatism. Beyond these we resort, in the establishment of probability, to experiment and observation and often find ourselves operating on insufficient inductions. Observation is limited, and experiment difficult to hedge about. We therefore resort to argument; and argument is of three kinds: first, argument from cause and effect or antecedent probability. We can argue from a man's character that he is going to look out for number one. We can argue from motives known or determinable, from opportunity, or from isolation, and in certain cases arrive at a degree of probability which it would be absurd to deny. The second class of arguments comes from analogy. We live by habit and habitual observation. Every day of our lives we act on analogical grounds in a thousand things, but analogy itself does not go far toward the establishment of the highest degree of probability. Our own proverb says, "It is always the unexpected which happens." This means that we notice the interruption of the course of habit, and that it does occur, this interruption. The third kind of argument, which arrives at the highest degree of probability where it applies or can be found, is the argument from sign. The argument from sign may be so highly probable as to be what we call incontestable. Argument from sign is in common use in finger-printing and in all circumstantial evidence. Defoe's *Shortest Way with Dissenters* is an argument from cause and effect presented in the form *a fortiori*. Burke makes powerful use of the argument from analogy in his *Conciliation with America*. There is much analogical argument in argumentative prose, particularly of the eighteenth century.

Aristotle insisted that all argument should be checked and purified of fallacies and gave a list of illusory or misleading arguments for the purpose of getting rid of them. Bacon agreed with Aristotle. The doctrine of the Idols is Bacon's contribution to the ascertainment of social and individual fallacies. These, he says, are the chief idols by which men go wrong: The first are Idols of the Tribe, fallacies or false notions of things incident to humanity, or the race in general. They are innate. The second are the Idols of the Cave, also innate, errors incident to the peculiar mental or bodily constitution of each individual. These are the innumerable fads or special interests of the particular man. The third are the Idols of the Forum or Market-place. They are not innate, but creep insensibly into men's minds as they live. As illustrations Bacon cites words, names, labels or slogans, party shibboleths, and social and economic clichés. The fourth are Idols of the Theater, fallacious methods of thinking thrust in upon us by false philosophies, erroneous methods of demonstration. Bacon has in mind the false philosophies of his own day: empirical, which from few and inadequate experiments leap to general conclusions, and superstitious, which corrupt philosophy by theological and poetical notions. I shall not of course pause to classify the fallacies to which I may call your attention in this course of lectures, but it is an easy exercise and one somewhat fraught with chagrin to find how perfectly identifiable our errors and delusions in American education are with Bacon's doctrine of the Idols.

It is obvious that we as humanists and students of literature have little directly to do with the demonstrations of the completely general, in other words, with objective proofs. These things may of course enter our field when they take on an individual or personal aspect. It is also clear that we are not greatly concerned with the practice of the social sciences. I am aware that we are in part, in large part, historians; but I think that does not make us social scientists, although we may under special circumstances become such. Indeed, we operate in the center of the concentric groups of which I spoke. How and why we operate I shall try to tell you in later lectures. I hope to justify our profession and hope to find certain guides to procedure within it. It is already clear that, of all seekers after truth, students of literature and art are most dependent on the determination of the probable, most liable to accept the part for the whole, the temporary for the eternal, and the prejudiced for the equitable. Art arises and subsists through feeling, and the ancients were right in perceiving an enmity between emotion and reason. We must, therefore, know the advantages as well as the disadvantages of our situation. We have arrived thus far at the hypothesis that probability in art and literature does not differ in essence from Bishop Butler's basis of prudential action.

In order that we may achieve a maximum of clarity, let us return for a little while to my three imaginary circles and apply our rubric to the familiar subject of the war effort. In the circle of the laboratory sciences the process of thought may exercise itself typically and to the full, a great advantage as regards definiteness and practicality. There man may pursue all the steps of thinking and may arrive at proof, which is the highest form of probability. The relation of work in physical science and technology to the war is so obvious as to require no comment, for a battle of science is now being waged whose story cannot be told until the war is over. We have pitted against us in this conflict the most ingenious and determined adversaries the world has ever known. It behooves us to do our best. The quest for new techniques, new weapons, new means of attack and defense is now incalculable both in scope and intensity. The best scientific brains of our own country and of our allies have been put to work by the Office of Scientific Research and Development in Washington and in London, and on their knowledge and efficiency depends very largely the outcome of the conflict. They are engaged on specific assignments and on general projects. Not the least important of their activities have to do with military medicine for the saving of the lives of those wounded in battle or smitten by disease. Men with scientific and technical ability are needed in great numbers by all arms of our fighting forces. So obviously important to this war effort are the works of technology, so immediate is the need and so comprehensible are the demands that many thinkers have concluded that the scientific branches of study are the only ones to which it is practical to devote our efforts in training and instruction for war.

The intermediate circle we decided was to represent the social sciences. They, too, often have, because of their situation, certain advantages in the search for definite truth. By means of the historical method and the statistical method; by means also of controlled observation and certain limited opportunities for experimentation, the social sciences are often able to arrive at high degrees of probability. Now only a moment's thought will suffice to convince us that the social sciences have a great part to play in this war. We have but to recall some of the economic, financial, and political questions that are or recently have been before us in the United States to see that expert knowledge and opinion in the social sciences may win the war for us and win the peace; and that, lacking such expert guidance and the spirit that is needed to implement it, we may yet suffer defeat in the war or in the peace that follows it. I have but to remind you of the enormous obscurity and the unpredictable difficulties which pervade and perplex international politics or of the threatening load of war debt in the field of national economics to convince you of the importance of the social sciences in this national effort. The science of war itself is a social science; so also are diplomacy, propaganda, government, education, labor relations, management, relief, transportation, finance, and the operations of the body politic. The service of the war requires not only those higher up in the control of social power, but also men and women of knowledge and skill in every rank and branch of national service.

It may seem that I have left almost nothing of importance to be attended to within the innermost circle of all, the circle of man himself as a single, separate creature; but such is not the case. There remains untouched perhaps the most important field of all. I know something about this field. I have spent my life in its exploitation. I know its relation to other fields. I know that man's cultural life is one and that it is as perilous for humanists to neglect science and social science as it is for scientists to neglect the humanities. I do not believe in a civil war among the differing but inevitable parts of human culture.

The chief characteristic of the humanities is that they and they alone in our academic scheme strive to speak to the individual man, immediately and directly. I put aside the silly idea that the humanities have to do with the beautification of life in favor of the idea that the humanities have to do with the living of life, a far broader and truer conception. As already indicated, the humanities present a difficult field in which to work. We can ordinarily not hope to arrive at proof in our determinations as do the natural scientists; and, because of the multifarious manifestations of individuality and the endless variety of individual qualities and motives, we cannot hope always or often to arrive at such high degrees of probability as may be achieved by the social scientists. Our importance is, however, not to be discounted because of our relation to proof and the highest degrees of probability. We are not blind leaders of the blind, but have many great and well tested instruments and policies provided for our use. We have, as the object of our study, man as an individual and a human being. We have the manifestation of man's instincts, biological and social. We have to guide us all that the philosophers, the psychologists, the anthropologists, the theologians, and the wise men of all ages have discovered about man in his warfare with his environment. We are concerned with all that has to do with man's behavior as a member of a social group and a family, or as a creature endowed with passion. We are concerned with his manners, his morals, and his intellect. We must carry our all-too-dim light into those regions left dark by the scientist and the social scientist. We deal with man's ambition, his love of country and home, his industry, and with his hope of salvation. It is we who have to teach the ideal of democracy and the dignity of man. It is we who might induce man the more readily to live for his country or to die for it.

We must, therefore, have a part to play in this mighty warfare and in the peace that follows it. Primarily let it be said that this war must be fought with soldiers. I was once a soldier myself, and you may be willing to listen to me. Who are the soldiers? I adapt a paragraph from J. B. Priestley in my effort to tell you who the soldiers are. The soldiers are real human beings. If you wound them, they bleed. They have fathers, mothers, sisters, brothers, sweethearts, wives and children. Like all men they swing between fear and hope. They have strange dreams. They hunger for happiness. They all have names and faces. They are not some cross-section of abstract human stuff. They are in the round and alive. And because they are real human beings, they can succeed or fail, they can be dutiful or slack, they can be cowardly or brave.

I know that this man, this fellow human being, this American soldier, should be spoken to by those who know how to speak to him, those who know the values and principles of our democracy. I know there are those, both living and dead, who can so speak. The love of home and country, the aspiration to play a man's part, the instincts for victory and self-defense arise naturally in the hearts of soldiers. The humanities are about them.

There are things about our history that our youth should know. In days of peace it may be salutary, as it is sometimes amusing, to engage in the pastime of debunking history; but, when the debunking is all done, the fact remains that our ancestors have conceived of, stated, fought for, and established the right to life, liberty, and the pursuit of happiness. The story goes back through Wilson, Lincoln, Washington and Jefferson, to Burke, Locke, Algernon Sidney, Milton, Tyndale, and Wyclif to the English Middle Ages. This spirit of liberty, this recognition of the rights and the dignity of man, is the reality back of our national life, however commercialized and frivolous our own life at times may appear to be. The essence of this spirit is embodied, consciously and unconsciously, in our literature. I believe that humanists—historians, philosophers, ministers of the gospel, students of the fine arts, and interpreters of literature—can and do support this war and that their support is essential. Let us in the universities, whose differences among ourselves, as I have tried to show, are negligible, present a united front.

Two points, neither developed at any great length in this lecture, I should like to leave with you for thoughtful consideration and future reference. The first is the necessity of guarding against fallacious thinking in all fields, particularly, I think, in the field of the humanities, where its inroads are almost unchecked. The second is the possibility of recognizing and achieving in the humanities a higher certainty to be based on a superior wisdom, that in turn growing out of straighter, clearer, better informed, and more catholic thinking.

CHAPTER II

THE POINT OF VIEW OF UNIVERSALITY

Now the weakness of these opinions may be shown, by observing the suppositions on which they are founded, which are really such as these:—that it cannot be thought God would have bestowed any favour at all upon us, unless in the degree which we think he might, and which, we imagine, would be most to our particular advantage; and also, that it cannot be thought he would bestow a favour upon any, unless he bestowed the same upon all: suppositions which we find contradicted, not by a few instances in God's natural government of the world, but by the general analogy of nature together.

SOME MONTHS ago there fell into my hands, through the kindness of Professor John W. Dodds, a document from the hands of Mr. Lewis Mumford in which he expressed tentatively some of the principles on which he meant to found his first course of lectures in the School of the Humanities at Stanford University. He spoke of t'ie whole nature of man as his object and of man as inseparable from nature and society. He deprecated a division between man's nature and his values, and between art and life. To this document I shall recur in a later paragraph of this lecture.

In my last lecture I laid the basis for what I am going to say in this one. You may recollect that I recommended, not only that scientists pay more attention to the humanities, but that humanists pay more attention to the organized knowledge of the social environment and to the stable conclusions of science. I regard that recommendation as aggressive, as an attack, although it may seem to many of you to be very mild or to be commonplace. I remind you of it for the sake of clarity and I remind myself of it because it seems on first sight to be a too extensive demand, quantitatively considered, and because it at once brings up the question of whether or not an effective qualitative standard can be maintained along with it.

Not only can an effective qualitative standard be maintained along with a greatly increased quantity to be learned in the pursuit of an education, but also the quality itself can be improved by that very means. We are too modest in our aims.

The mind is capable of far greater reaches than our indolent theories permit us to assert. It is stated on an authority for which I do not vouch, although I believe in the general truth of the idea, that the possible synaptic connections within the human brain amount to about three billion, and that the "ordinary" educated mind achieves about three million. In other words, it lives up to about one one-thousandth of its possibilities. This is certainly no very high achievement, and, whether these rather wild-sounding figures are even approximately correct or not, nobody doubts that the ordinary educated man is but a fragment of an Aristotle, a Bacon, or a Newton. Certainly by setting our educational standards higher we cannot fail to accomplish more.

Let me illustrate my meaning from the current practice of specialization, and, in order that my attack may not seem to be invidious, let me draw my illustrations from my own field. A practice which makes and then respects narrow specialties in modern literary fields is hardly short of absurd. Why should any man's specialty be limited to the sixteenth, seventeenth, eighteenth, nineteenth, or twentieth century in English literature? To set the Romantic Movement or the Age of Queen Anne off as an exclusive domain is to narrow and abridge the conception of those periods, and to divide the subject of American literature up into Colonial literature, Early National literature, the Flowering of New England, and American literature since 1870 is to take, not two bites, but four bites, to a cherry. This has nothing to do with the convenient practice of the setting aside of chronological groups to be handled in units comprehensible by students and teachers in single terms or semesters, nor does it deny that only limited amounts of data can be held effectively in the mind at any one time. It is a matter of the qualifications, the authoritative qualifications, of the scholar in the whole field. For temporary purposes, such as writing books and articles and directing research, it may not be convenient for professors at any one time to brighten up and review their knowledge of numerous particular periods and particular authors; but surely there is nothing recondite or unduly arduous about it. Any well trained English scholar in a few weeks or months of comparative leisure ought to be, and usually is, able to write books and learned articles and to direct research in any of these literary fields, which, moreover, are so much a unified whole that he cannot afford completely to neglect any of them. Let us keep, if you like, the prevailing partitions as conveniences, but let us not conceive of them as barriers or as marking off self-contained units.

It would be beneficial and pleasant in carrying on the work of college English teachers to exchange courses frequently. All teachers of English literature should be specialists in Shakespeare, and the interesting thing about it is that most of them are; and it is not well for English teachers to be out of touch with Spenser, Milton, Wordsworth, and other great formative geniuses. In point of fact, it is not usually a matter of ignorance, although it might become so, but of oblivescence. The process of recall is easy and delightful, and the method of the scholar carries over readily. Let us preserve, not only the purity, but also the richness and scope of our subject. If we do so, we shall work with a more effective sense of proportion and with less pretense and pedantry. With reference to Old English and Middle English, I might well be more concessive, for a great deal of obscure material has to be held actively in mind in working within these fields, and partition may be justified; but, to be frank with you, I would not go too far. The distinction between Renaissance and Middle Ages is largely factitious, and no man does well in Renaissance literature who does not have Chaucer and the Middle Ages within easy recall. I would not, moreover, set my colleagues in English free from a continual study of literary art as art, or from the study of foreign literatures, ancient and modern, or from history, philosophy, and the thought and spirit of our own age. It is threatened that we may become like Bishop Berkeley's "Critic fly" on the pillar of St. Paul's, "whose prospect was confined to a little part of one of the stones . . . the joint beauty of the whole or the distinct use of its parts were inconspicuous, and nothing could appear but the small inequalities in the surface of the hewn stone, which in the view of that insect seemed so many deformed rocks and precipices."

In thus making an attack on the home front, I do not profess humility, for everybody knows that it is not we in the field of English who are the worst offenders in this absurd, unnecessary, and unrelated kind of specialization. We are no doubt bad enough, but my point is that it is certainly not required that any of us should embrace voluntary poverty. It is not obligatory that the boy in school should choose between manual training and bookkeeping, on the one hand, and liberal studies, on the other, for the answer is "both." The present tendency reminds me of Emerson's "Days":

Daughters of Time, the hypocritic Days,
Muffled and dumb like barefoot dervishes,
And marching single in an endless file,
Bring diadems and fagots in their hands.
To each they offer gifts after his will,
Bread, kingdoms, stars, and sky that holds them all.
I, in my pleached garden, watched the pomp,
Forgot my morning wishes, hastily
Took a few herbs and apples, and the Day
Turned and departed, silent. I, too late,
Under her solemn filet saw the scorn.

To those who protest that this idea I have expressed puts too heavy a burden on the mind and the memory, I have something to say by way of rejoinder. Nobody could have a lower and more regretful opinion of the memories of our current students than I have. They usually do not know who Grover Cleveland and Andrew Jackson were, and yet they have studied American history and must have heard of these not inconspicuous or uninteresting persons. It is so with regard to many important persons and important facts. One is forced to conclude that these students have not been made to learn things, to train their memories and to exercise the simpler processes of thought. This is evident also from their frequent lack of any chronological or sequential principle of organization in their mental make-up. If they know that Shakespeare and Chaucer are both dead, they do not know which of them lived first within a hazy period of the whole past. They do not know any historical difference between King David of Israel and the Apostle Paul. They have not been induced to memorize psalms or commandments or great poems, passages, or proverbs, and in that neglect they have missed a great deal in the betterment of their minds, their vocabularies, and their sense of English style. The ignorance or indifference of parents is no doubt partly responsible for this unfortunate situation.

There is also a widely current educational theory which must bear its share of the blame. According to this theory little children in school, if left to follow their own untrammeled desires, will naturally seek enlightenment. This is at best a romance shot through with wishful thinking; at worst it is perhaps a mad desire to gain personal distinction by advocating revolution and reform. Nobody but Dogberry has ever said that reading and writing come by nature. Essentially the theory is bad science and in its operation socially deleterious and uneconomical. Book learning is not in the course of nature. Nature does not and cannot interest itself directly in those possibilities of the brain which concern us as teachers of the corpus of civilized learning. And awakening social compulsion is not yet strong enough to bring education about. In so far as our students are worthy of better treatment, and all of them potentially are, it is a pity that they should be neglected; but beyond a certain point they are, when they come to us, already in the purlieus of utter darkness. Many of them seem strangely deficient in curiosity. They do not know that kangaroos come from Australia, and they do not care. If a student with an active brain should for the first time get acquainted with a kangaroo, he would say, unless restrained by politeness, "Where in the world did you come from, and what have you got in your pocket?" I am willing to go this far, "All men naturally desire knowledge, but not all men desire the labor of learning." And to those who discount my program for English study as non-comprehensible, I would suggest that they rouse up their energy and throw half a million more brain-cells into the job of learning.

The ideal of all people who aspire to the education of the faculties, whether that ideal is fully achieved or not, should be one of effectiveness and breadth. The immediate task is the rescue of the individual from the narrow innermost circle of self, the ultimate task is the realization of self in relation to environment. The youth must be taught consciously to remember, to judge of differences and similarities, to assume points of view and entertain hypotheses, to arrive ultimately at the ability to perceive unity in variety, and to exercise the full abilities of a trained intelligence. I have chosen on this occasion to present these things under the aspect of universality.

I wish to relate these speculations about universality on which we are now engaged to the doctrine of probability which I developed in my first lecture. In so doing I make use of certain ideas about criticism which I gained by the reading of an un-published work by Professor Myron F. Brightfield of the University of California. In order to bring the matter before you, let me quote again from Bishop Butler, author of the famous *Analogy*. He says in his careful, sober way, "The practical question in all cases is, whether the evidence for a course of action be such, as, taking in all circumstance, makes the faculty within us, which is the guide and judge of conduct, determine that course of action to be prudent. Indeed, satisfaction that it will be for our interest or happiness, abundantly determines an action to be prudent; but evidence almost infinitely lower than this determines actions to be so too; even in the conduct of every day." If I understand Professor Brightfield correctly, he proposes this principle of probability, broadly conceived, as a controlling factor in determining the value of literature and art. If this is true, the effect would be to integrate art and life and to make of art an inseparable aspect of life. I wish to warn you against taking the value found in art to be a merely moral value or devoid of a moral value. It must be in some sense truth to life, and I believe this truth to life is the ultimate basis of all artistic as well as moral satisfaction. I present the idea to you undogmatically as worthy of consideration.

It will be seen that Bishop Butler employs the logical doctrine of probability explained in our first lecture in the determination of truth as a basis for prudential action as well as for religious belief. This same principle would thus become a norm of human life of the utmost universality. Professor Brightfield contends, I think wisely, that the greatest and most enduring literature observes this norm and operates within the limits of the probable. If so, the greatest literature becomes a guide of life. What further relation this idea has to the distinction between the probable and the improbable in art, a distinction going back to Aristotle, I shall not now inquire, although I think the ideas are reconcilable. Let us illustrate the issue from Dr. Johnson.

Dr. Johnson in his life of the poet Gray in the *Lives of the Poets* (Bohn ed., III, 381-2) says somewhat prejudicially of Gray's "The Bard," "To select a singular event and swell it to a giant's bulk by fabulous appendages of spectres and predictions, has little difficulty, for he that forsakes the probable may always find the marvelous. And it has little use; we are affected only as we believe; we are improved only as we find something to be imitated or declined." Without any intention of being tied up to Dr. Johnson's hostility to the romantic or his prejudice against the poet Gray, I submit that Dr. Johnson has here reflected an interesting hypothesis. To give satisfaction, literature, or the criticism of life presented by literary works, must carry the conviction of being probable. According to this hypothesis an improbable work may give local and temporary or delusive gratification but can have little lasting value as art. What is needed, and what great critics supply, is inductive determination of relatively permanent values.

I take it that there is nothing essentially mystical in the critic's function, and I do not believe that there is evidence of divine inspiration among critics as such. I am rather disposed to take the Crocean point of view. All works of the past and of the present are theoretically capable of projecting themselves into the region of contemporary appreciation, although only a relatively small number actually do so. I have been interested in Croce's restoration to intelligibility and vitality of many minor Italian writers of the Renaissance, writers who were otherwise dumb and speechless. Every reader who knows the literature of the past and is able to overcome the difficulties in the way of its comprehension adds to his books and his friends, and so brings the dead to life. It is Croce's idea that a critic properly qualified by knowledge and sympathy confronts a work of art with, theoretically speaking, a perfectly endowed and equipped personality, goes through an imaginary experience, and recreates the work of art. This lays a great burden on the critic, but it does not segregate him from other readers of books, for he has done, more purposefully, exactly what an ordinary reader does when he reads a book of literature. The reader also assesses the value of the work in terms of the entire framework of his humanistic knowledge. Such knowledge may be great or small, as likewise his ability, but he looks at each work he reads as an hypothesis or speculation about life. If he does not like the work, he usually does not read it, or, if he does read it, he does not recommend it to others. He confronts literature with life. If his criticism is hampered by ignorance or prejudice, if he is not honest in his motive, so that he seeks flattery or escape instead of truth, his criticism is to that extent invalid; but, by and large, his criticism is determinant. According to this theory, variations from the norm of probability are always in the direction of the false, for the path of great literature is always the open road of truth to life. Even when there is an improbable proviso or an unwarranted presupposition about the nature of things, as in Swift's *Gulliver's Travels* or Cervantes' *Don Quixote*, the true literary artist always returns to and proceeds along the highway of truth. To be adequate to his task and useful to his fellow men, the critic must be a specialist in the goals of beauty, the recognition of truth, and the determination of the prospective satisfactions of man alive in the world. In thus making of the critic a citizen of the world we ennoble his function and broaden the conception of his activity. The great critic becomes an ordinary man endowed with extraordinary powers and not a wizard, or an oracle, or a showman. We thus extend his function to the breadth of humanity, and this is likewise our ideal as we talk of the extension of our minds.

We must not refuse to apply our doctrine of probability to our doctrine of versatility. Just to what degree were Leonardo, Galileo, and Newton exceptional? Or shall we say Leeuwenhoek, Johnson, and Pasteur, or Darwin, Steinmetz, and T. E. Lawrence? Shall we think of them as mutations without power of reproduction and conceive of them in relation to the world under the figure of an obelisk with low base and high central shaft? I think not. I prefer the figure of a pyramid to represent them and their fellow men. I believe that the middle distance between the apex and the base is also filled with men of intellectual power and that all men have, in relative degrees, realized and unrealized possibilities. The Elizabethans in large numbers and no doubt the Athenians of the age of Pericles sought for and achieved both versatility and eminence. Bacon proudly took the whole field of learning as his province, and there are significant cases of men and nations nearer at hand. If we had but the courage to try it out, we too might rise higher in the scale of being and achievement.

As to possibilities for the future, it is immediately obvious that, if our aims are low, our achievements are not likely to be high. At this time the war stands like a great curtain before us, but I think some light may be derived from our experience in the field of education after the first world war, and it is likely that many of the conditions which then existed will again arise after the end of the present war. After the first world war many men hoped for a renaissance of art and learning. They based their hope, not so much on a study of the signs of the times, as on logical process. Such a displacement of accepted ideas, such an infraction of habit, such a stimulation of mind and heart must, they thought, be followed by regeneration. Such things had happened before. The struggle with Spain, when the Armada was beaten, scattered, and wrecked along the coasts of the western islands, had been followed by Shakespeare, Spenser, and Bacon. The upheaval of the French Revolution had given us Wordsworth, Byron, and Victor Hugo. The fact or sense of victory itself was elation and a trumpet call to action and endeavor. But the manifestations of the new life were none too obvious. Mr. Ramsay

Muir and other critics saw signs of an awakening spirit in art and letters, but it cannot be said that these signs were fulfilled.

Those of us who came back from the war were surprised, but possibly not displeased, to find the world pretty much the same one we had left; and we were conscious of creating some disappointment in our communities by our eagerness to take up the old tasks and live the old lives. And yet our young people flocked to the universities. We began in many places to number our freshmen by the thousand. The students were largely without plan or purpose and were less, rather than more, assured of their proper course than were those who came to us in the older days. They thus presented an opportunity for guidance and inspiration. The responsibility resting upon institutions of higher learning was enormous. They were slow to take advantage of it, but they did the best they could. There were, I think, two reasons why we partly failed. Our ideals were wrong, and the tide of worldliness was too heavy for us to stem. On the one hand, we had come to believe in our own heresies and to be sure we knew what should be done and were so efficient in our guidance that we sometimes had the misfortune to have our theories carried out in practice. American education had been for more than a generation a believer in specialization, and we had by that time reshaped our college courses to provide for it. We had told our young men to find one thing to do, not one thing to become, one profession or business to select, one prize to strive for, and we told them to press forward toward this goal like the runner in the Epistle to the Philippians. The Apostle's injunction to quench not the spirit, but to prove all things was not sufficiently heeded. We needed an ideal of enlightened versatility in the development of the individual student, and we had instead an ideal of rather selfish specialization, an ideal of getting on, which quickly led to an ideal of "getting by."

We might have done much, and much yet remains to be done, to make each subject yield its vision or pattern of creative activity, even when persons pursuing such subjects do not feel narrowly affected in their personal interests. We saw our job in worldly terms and usually not *sub specie aeternitatis*. All university subjects have their appeal to normal minds, and that college student who is told or suffered to think that he is not doing anything yet and that he will begin to live only when, having collected such and such number of academic credits, he may begin his life's work, has his eyes blinded and his ears stopped. This business of higher education either means something or it does not. I think it ought to mean something.

I should like for you to consider with me in this connection this proposition: the total effect of the advancement of science and the liberal studies has been, not to make the field of fundamental learning more difficult and quantitatively more extensive, but, actually for practical purposes, easier and less extensive. The text books in physics and chemistry now used in high schools contain enough physics for a physicist and enough chemistry for a chemist. What Newton and Boyle knew is as nothing compared to what we put into the hands of children. The extension of the field of knowledge is thought of at first sight as a vast increase in the student's burden; whereas, the truth is quite the contrary. So many things have been rendered definite and intelligible which were formerly mysterious and perplexing that the modern student is relatively rich in time as well as in opportunity. Knowledge and art lie before him literally like an open book. Indeed, the modern school and college student shows his wealth of leisure in his habits. Having been assured that only one sort of culture concerns him, and often not the whole of it, he shuts his mind to the rest. Time hangs heavy on his hands. Why therefore should we discourage avocations in one breath and in the next lament the enormous waste of time which students expend in courting or in going to the movies? The industrious youth becomes as quickly as possible a specialist, or a misfit in a specialty, and the idler whiles away his time in mere amusement. Our course of study from the kindergarten through the university is easy, and we have to repeat a lot of things to make it last to the end. The thing that might put vitality into it all along the line is an ideal of many-sided culture.

Who therefore would not fear that the youth flocking into our colleges after the war, seeking they know not what vague blessing, may be misguided? (We must also remember that they will often or usually not ask our advice but will ask the advice of other knowing students.) Told, for example, to pursue some narrow aim and taught that nothing in all the great curriculum concerns them save only that, they will seek no fair field for the exercise of their natural powers. To have them turn aside, their capacities untried, the realms of human achievement still unknown, with no friends among the arts, no participation in the thought of the race, no vision of men and manners of men overseas or long ago, is a calamity for which no minor specialized skill can compensate. To pursue a more humane policy does not mean that they will become, if they so desire, less efficient specialists, but quite the contrary. Men of ability are forever demonstrating the adaptability of human intelligence. If a man is great in one thing he can usually achieve greatness in a group of related things or even in quite different things. The ideal of the completest possible self-realization is always salutary, for the old as well as for the young. I would not be unreasonable. Cato the Elder is said to have learned Greek at the age of eighty. I favor the undertaking and admire Cato's courage, but I think that eight rather than eighty is the proper age to begin Greek. I recognize, nevertheless, special talent and do not think it should be interfered with by extraneous requirements. Indeed, I have always admired the saying attributed to Themistocles: "I cannot fiddle, but I can make a small city into a great state."

The ideal of the all-round man has been unconsciously accepted in our colleges, although frequently the varied offerings of the college course form but a small arc in the circle. Certain men become heroes and idols in their institutions, because, with some standing in their classes, they are also athletes and public men. The general practice is gratifying, and, were the ideal recognized as a valid one, it ought to be possible in this age to secure in many men a better rounded intellectual development by a freer and more natural participation in the varied activities of the arts and sciences. The one most lamentable thing is the early choice of a narrow goal. It is a sign of weakness, sometimes greed, in higher institutions to encourage it, since it tends to shape our youth according to pattern and subsequently to deliver them to be sold like merchandise.

It may even be said that these highly practical devices prove in the end to be highly impractical. You will find no word about doing one exclusive thing in all the wisdom of Poor Richard. It was Franklin's idea that a man should strive and thrive in order that he might have time to invent lamp-posts, lightning-rods, and constitutions. John Dryden was sneering at one of the most brilliant and interesting men of his age when he said that Zimri seemed to be "not one, but all mankind's epitome."

What we really seek in speaking thus crudely in favor of versatility is to amplify our own souls and the souls of our pupils. "That one man should die ignorant who had the capacity for knowledge," said Carlyle, "this I call a tragedy, were it to happen more than twenty times in the minute, as by some computations it does." It makes small difference what courses a student takes in college, but his attitude, his morals, and his mind make all the difference in the world.

The other reason I suggest for our at least partial failure after the first world war is that there appeared in our society at that time a powerful group of rivalries and diversions, so powerful that I think no body of academicians could have withstood them. We then had in common use the automobile, and our students began to roar about the country. We had also the movies and the radio, and the minds of our students became diffused. They lost or never acquired the powers of memory and concentration. About that time began the mad exploitation of business and of organized amusement. The faculty became ridiculous and oldfashioned to students who quite naturally found Hollywood with its jazz bands more attractive than college professors busy in their libraries and laboratories. Students took over our institutions and restated, with the help of certain academical fifth-columnists and quislings, our ideals for us. We fought, on the whole, a good fight, and we got something out of it. Many fine buildings, which still stand, were constructed. It was an era of brick and stone and of intellectual defeat.

When we think about the post-war world, let us strive to be as reasonable and as completely realistic as we can. We have much ground to regain. We must strive to recapture our institutions of learning from idle, ignorant persons. We may fail, and we may well be beaten again, for our enemies have not visibly lost power, and our own forces have not yet been greatly augmented. We shall nevertheless have some advantages, and national suffering and post-war adversity may do something to bring our people to their senses, just as the depression helped us while it lasted.

Bacon has some surprising and rather encouraging things to say about the effects of adversity: "It was a high speech of Seneca (after the manner of Stoics), that the good things which belong to prosperity are to be wished; but the good things that belong to adversity are to be admired, *Bona rerum secundarum optabilia; adversarum mirabilia.*" The world's ideal of prosperity rises only to the status of desirability; whereas the much dreaded condition of adversity rises to the production of admirable things. "The pencil of the Holy Ghost," Bacon says, "hath labored more in

describing the afflictions of Job than the felicities of Solomon."
He goes further and adds that "prosperity doth best discover
[that is, reveal to us] vice, but adversity doth best discover
virtue."

It is evident that we must confront a world badly in need of
redintegration. As Mr. Mumford puts it in another connection,
we must suggest "the new shapes of personality demanded of our
generation for our survival and renewal." I have suggested the
need for broadly trained men and women capable of directing
wisely these processes of survival, also the need for balance
between the outer and inner worlds. I have suggested a unified
approach to knowledge and life and a braver, more hopeful attempt
at mastery. I have asked for recognition by all of us including
the scientists themselves of a fuller significance of the advancement of science. This I have done and have made a puzzled
acknowledgment that our fundamental assumptions about nature
and man are and may continue to be derivations by society. It is
certainly true—and I see in it a point of attack on humanistic
problems—that civilization rests, in Mr. Mumford's words, "on a
series of masterly inventions both political and technical," and I
think also that these fundamental inventions may be artistic and
moral as well as political and technical. And yet the ultimate
in our effort as educators is not society but the individual man.
I have urged also that there be no divorce between the humane
and the practical aspects of living. Like Mr Mumford, I have
urged our need for order, intelligibility, and purpose. I have
urged also both an amplification and an intensification of education by effort, memory, and discipline. It is written that "the
letter killeth and the spirit giveth life," and far be it from me to
recommend or to follow any course of action which is not motivated
by the spirit and is not addressed to the spirit rather than to the
time or the material or the intellectually abstract. It may be that
in the providence of God we shall pass through this crisis in our
spiritual history, and in the meantime all that we can do, and it is
perhaps enough, is to say *In manus tuas, O Domine!* and to keep
our eyes fastened on the guiding light.

> Set where the upper streams of Simois flow
> Was the Palladium, high 'mid rock and wood;
> And Hector was in Ilium, far below,
> And fought and saw it not—but there it stood.

It stood, and sun and moonshine rained their light
On the pure columns of its glen-built hall.
Backward and forward rolled the waves of fight
Round Troy—but while this stood, Troy could not fall.

So, in its lovely moonlight, lives the soul.
Mountains surround it and sweet virgin air;
Cold-plashing, past it, crystal waters roll;
We visit it by moments, ah, too rare!

We shall renew the battle on the plain
Tomorrow; red with blood will Xanthus be;
Hector and Ajax will be there again,
Helen will come upon the wall to see.

Then shall we rust in shade, or shine in strife,
And fluctuate 'twixt blind hopes and blind despairs,
And fancy that we put forth all our life,
And never know how with the soul it fares.

Still doth the soul from its lone fastness high,
Upon our life a ruling effluence send.
And when it fails, fight as we will, we die;
And while it lasts we cannot wholly end.

I have read you this poem as an expression of an enduring, intuitional, albeit somewhat Calvinistic, faith that we need not strive in vain to find a solution for our problem of reviving the spiritual life of our country. I have pointed in this lecture in one large and as yet rather vague direction in which I think we ought to proceed, the direction, namely, of a more extensive and catholic aim in the acquisition of knowledge. In later lectures I should like to explore with you various roads and trails which I think will lead, if not to the celestial city, at least to regions nearer the land of promise. I believe we can succeed.

Wisdom, beauty, and truth seem always to be appreciated by those who behold them; indeed, seem to have, as Aristotle thought, a clear title to superiority over the vices, which are their opposites. Yet everywhere we look we see a readiness on the part of many people to follow gladly the frivolous or foolish, the ugly, the false, and even the cowardly. Can we ascertain why this is? And if we can, what is our means of salvation? What I have suggested that we might use is the cultivation of superior intelligence. Can we help to provide it, or rescue normal intelligence from waste more abundantly than we do now? The objective of an increase in knowledge is an increase in power and control, and on this principle we rest our case.

CHAPTER III

THE IMAGINATIVE POINT OF VIEW

Thus people habituate themselves to let things pass through their minds, as one may speak, rather than to think of them. Thus by use they become satisfied merely with seeing what is said, without going any further. Review and attention, and even forming a judgment, becomes fatigue; and to lay anything before them that requires it, is putting them quite out of their way.

THE WORD "imaginative" suggests clearly enough the aspect of humanistic study which I now wish to bring to your attention. I chose it because of my familiarity with the rôle assigned to the image-making power of the mind in older literature. The word "imagination" has for me a rather rich connotation, for imagination in the old faculty psychology was both the hero and the villain of the mental kingdom. In Shakespeare's time and since, the meaning of the word has been pretty much what it is now. We still know exactly what Shapespeare means when he says:

> And as imagination bodies forth
> The forms of things unknown, the poet's pen
> Turns them to shapes, and gives to airy nothing
> A local habitation and a name.

Particularly since the time of Wordsworth and Coleridge the tendency has been fairly stable in regarding imagination as a shaping or modifying agency and in using it especially to denote the plastic or creative power of the mind. It is still defined as the reorganization of data derived from past experience, with new relations, into a present ideational experience. Imagination is primarily the power or process of having mental images, and, more broadly, the power or process of forming ideal constructions from images, concepts, and feelings, with a reference to past, present, or future, and with relative freedom from objective restraint. The psychologists apply to imagination such qualifying words as "reproductive," "productive," and "creative."

Memory is defined as a generic term for those experiences, movements, or functions which are conditioned upon earlier experiences, movements, or functions of the organism. The essential characteristic of memory is retention, but it may also include reproduction. The two processes of memory and imagination are very close together. The exactness and vividness of both memory and imagination depend largely on our ability to observe our perceptions exactly, and slovenly observation is perhaps the original sinner in most of the many tragedies of education. Perception must be trained, and memory must be especially exercised, for memory is a responsible citizen of the world. Memory has even a wider utility than imagination; for it is essential for every man to learn to distinguish definitely between truth and falsehood. Bearing false witness for whatever reason is forbidden, and memory has had a commandment put in charge of it. The whole subject, however, of the training of perception, the awakening and maintenance of interest and attention, and the achievement of mnemonic reliability, I pass over as sufficiently well known and as beyond my purpose, as also the physical limitations of perception (and therefore of memory and imagination) and likewise the possible dependence of all men on the inheritance of associational tracts in the brain.

I am interested, however, in a discrimination in higher education between mere reproduction and the modification of data within the mind, a modification which we sometimes call thinking and by which we sometimes mean activity of the imagination. Without denying the utility of mere verbal thinking, one would insist in the pursuit of higher education on the cultivation of exact and vivid imagination, a thing which is serviceable in all occupations and essential in creative activities and in all dealings with the unknown. In other words and more simply, one would insist that, when college students have taken into their minds bodies of fact and opinion, they should if possible be induced to modify them in some fashion before they are poured out again. Dr. Woodrow Wilson used to say, with reference to the common practice of pouring information into students and then requiring them to reproduce it exactly in their examinations, that, although he regarded it as an intellectual exercise, he regarded it as the lowest form of such activity.

In any incursions I may make into the realm of psychology I would not talk nonsense. I realize that the matters I am trying to simplify are extremely complicated. I know that the mind is one, and, in spite of my habituation to a literature impregnated with faculty psychology, an erroneous and outmoded system, I really think of the mind as one even when I speak of its various aspects as if they were separable parts. I recognize within my purpose the necessity of stirring the emotions or sometimes of controlling them. I know the nature of reason in which an abstracted character is made to suggest consequences. I am interested in the development of that process. My real aim is the perception of essence, or sagacity, which operates for me as an agent in a world which proceeds on the basis, not of proof, but of probability. I know that this is often called by the name of faith. I have already talked to you in an elementary fashion about belief, which I should like to see supplemented by a superior intelligence. I apprehend even the concealed rôle played by instinct, either primitive or sublimated, and I am aware of the incredibly varied issues of experience in what we regard as necessary truths. I would not distort the picture, and I shall try not to do so.

In practice I have used and seen used the expression "freeing the mind," and I have wondered as to the nature of the process and have not thought the word "freeing" a satisfactory word unless we understand it as not only freeing, but also awakening and actually creating a mind. I bring to my assistance in this perplexity an illustration from John Milton which will perhaps supply us with an interpretation of the word "freedom" of which in this connection we can approve. Milton's conception of liberty or freedom was not a static one, not a mere cutting away of bonds and restrictions. He thought of the freedom of the individual as a positive, generative process. He thought that the condition of freedom bred virtue of every sort from age to age in a people who possessed it, and the history of free societies seems to show that he was right. Troubles have come to both Britain and America when the freedom of our peoples has been restricted, and states, not Rome only, have decayed when they have lost their liberty. Therefore, when I speak of imagination as an agency for setting free the minds of students, I mean more than mere emancipation, more than an attack on this, that, or the other restrictive convention or routine pattern of thought. We are entirely familiar with the idol-breaking activities of Mencken and Shaw, Joyce and Proust, Eliot and Hemingway, and dozens of other modernists including the wholesale rejections of the current illuminati. These iconoclasts may often be right. They may even be justifiable. But the ideal I have formed for freeing the mind includes them in its circumference and even goes beyond them, for it is one which would be so far enlightened that it would assess rightly the origin, nature, and utility of conventions and models of thought. There is nothing sensational about my ideal, which is strictly objective and inclusive and would and does prove itself effective.

Take, for example, Darwinism in thought. In the later nineteenth and earlier twentieth centuries Darwinism affected practically every field of social thinking and was, by and large, a fruitful concept. It is still an active and, I think, a productive mode of thought. But when it was used as Karl Marx used it, as an absolute and without the qualifications with which Charles Darwin had hedged it about, and thus made to account for and justify a great many things to which it did not and could not well apply, it became the Idol of the Market-place, productive of error then and now. The Darwinian hypothesis as enunciated and limited by Darwin is still accepted in the field of animal biology, but it breaks down when it is carried into fields whose operations are not biological. Brunetière in *L'Evolution des genres dans l'histoire de la littérature* (1890) wrote volumes on the evolution of literature or volumes which presupposed that literature was subject to Darwin's principles. More than thirty years ago the late Professor John Matthews Manly, dissatisfied with the erroneous results of the application of Darwinian evolution to literature, hit upon an ingenious and effective means of combatting it. The Dutch botanist Hugo De Vries had by that time developed his theory of mutation in species (*The Mutation Theory*, 1901) according to which new species come into existence, not by slow process of differentiation, but by sudden and unaccountable jumps in the historical chain of birth and reproduction. The probability of this theory had been widely accepted, and the shrewd idea occurred to Manly that, if Darwin's theory of evolution had some application to the history of literature, so also might De Vries's theory of mutation have. The result was Manly's epoch-making article in *Modern Philology* (IV, 1907, 577-95) entitled "Literary Forms and the Origin of Species," in which he showed that the appearance of new forms in the field of literature was analogous to the theory of De Vries rather than to that of Darwin. Human invention seemed to correspond to the jump which produced the new species in the biological chain. Manly did not make the mistake of declaring his discovery a universal rule, but called attention to the fact that in both cases we have to do, not with a fundamental law arising within the literary field itself, but with analogy drawn from a different field.

In somewhat the same way, I have no doubt that the extreme doctrine of art for art's sake has been stimulating and useful in the literary world, although I am still disposed to believe it a logical hypothesis whose end is pure mechanism and that there is and must always be in every human work a coloration of significance and that the approximate absence of moral or personal bias is itself a coloration. With reference to communism as a goal of evolution, I am disposed to deny both the identity of the goal and the evidence pointing to progression in its direction. These attitudes, which I believe to be both intelligent and fearless, are very different from those of fanatical advocates, wanton destroyers, and hidebound conservatives. I believe that an attempt at the completest possible understanding and the broadest and truest possible interpretation is in line with the practice of the best minds, ancient and modern, and that this attempt may be said to epitomize the function of the university in the modern world. I believe it is a free attitude and one that is naturally assumed by a free and courageous mind. I should like to promote this freedom of mind among my students, whose conclusions, let it be said, need not agree with mine.

I have thought also of this emancipation in terms of escape from the narrow world of self. No doubt it is biologically necessary that the young should be exceedingly selfish, and they often go, it seems to me, further than biology demands. The Apostle says, "When I was a child, I spoke as a child, I understood as a child, I thought as a child: but when I became a man, I put away childish things" (I Cor. iv. 11). And the putting away of childish things seems to be in some measure a matter of seeing the world with other than selfish eyes. Falling in love, for example, seems to be an almost divinely instituted means of teaching young men that they are not the sole possessors of interest and importance in the world. Note how Shakespeare marks the point in Romeo's life when his really strong and noble character came, so to speak, into existence at a single bound. Romeo says to a servingman,

> What lady is that, which doth enrich the hand
> Of yonder knight?

The servingman replies, "I do not know, sir," and Romeo says,

> O, she doth teach the torches to burn bright!
> It seems she hangs upon the cheek of night

Like a rich jewel in an Ethiope's ear;
Beauty too rich for use, for earth too dear!
So shows a snowy dove trooping with crows,
As yonder lady o'er her fellows shows.
The measure done, I'll watch her place of stand,
And, touching hers, make blessed my rude hand.
Did my heart love till now? Forswear it, sight!
For I ne'er saw true beauty till this night.

Alas! for those who never fall in love, whose hearts are never drawn out of themselves, those who, by dint of spoiling in childhood and youth, proceed in their solemn and sullen selfishness to a lifetime spent in acquisitiveness and the gratification of appetite! It is here that literature becomes a powerful force in the education of the young, for it may by appeal to the imagination bring it about that the young interest themselves in the lives, thoughts, and fates of others. I have always believed that, if we can get our hard, self-absorbed young people to be genuinely sorry for Romeo and Juliet, or indignant in their behalf, the seeds of a kinder life are already sown. Oliver Twist's request for more has perhaps bettered the feeding of many children, and no man who has understood Hamlet can ever be so obnoxiously cocksure of himself as he was before. Humor too, as well as pathos, beauty, and fellow feeling, is an agency in the rescue of youth from itself.

I should like also to see brought about in our students a habit of awareness, an anticipation of significance in terms of the past. It would assist our students to form a concept of themselves, of their already established characters, of their fathers and families also, and of the race to which they belong and from which they are descended. My own rearing in the South was, in some respects, almost patriarchal, and I think that no small part of the best in me and my schoolmates was our sense of who we were. Literature again comes to our aid, but perhaps nothing can take the place of self-respecting and respect-compelling parents. As our population settles into place and lives for generations in the same localities, is there not some hope that pride in family will again assert itself and that there will again be those in large numbers whose joy it is to carry on from generation to generation the honorable name and conduct of families?

The imagination must also be called into play in order that the young may become truly aware of the present, of the immediate bearings of an act, a thought, or a situation. It is thus that a feeling of responsibility and a sense of duty may come into existence, as also an anticipation of social consequences. The young are still sensitive to eloquence, if they can be induced to listen, and we do not preach to them effectively enough. Shakespeare and the Elizabethans believed in the power of the spoken word; they were a youthful people, and they were not wrong. Young people still respond to the eloquence of Shakespeare, and I can remember, as no doubt you can, having my heart stirred as with a trumpet by the urgent plea of Ulysses to Achilles in *Troilus and Cressida*, although I think the first great sermon I found in books was Burns's "Epistle to a Young Friend."

Finally, I have thought of the development of an imaginative point of view whose reference is future. All young people, all people as far as I know, are interested in their own personal trends and their own futures. This is a worthy objectification, and it is no very long step that they have to take to become interested in the future of their families, their friends, even of outsiders, or indeed of the race. Surely, the beginnings of life, or the approaches of old age and death, are sufficiently arrestive.

In order to make any great headway in college it is necessary that students should know how to read. Many students do not. I do not refer to the enormous numbers of illiterates revealed by the draft. I refer to high school graduates and to students in college. And if I were responsible for the program of a college, I would institute tests and start reading classes, for the thing is essential. Many of our students in college can write their names and spell out a few words, but are actually unable to get the sense from a page of even simple printed matter. Earlier this year I met my colleague at the University of North Carolina, a distinguished professor of education, on his way to post more than five thousand letters addressed to applicants who had been examined for admission to college as V-12's and had failed. It was this gentleman's task to administer in the Southeastern States the examinations set by the U. S. Government for prospective V-12's. There will probably be more than a hundred thousand high school graduates and college students rejected, and the examiner told me that an overwhelming majority of those who fail do so because they are unable to read and understand the questions they are asked. These people come to college and are somehow permitted to slip through in large numbers, just as they have slipped through in high school.

There is no use in talking to such people about literary culture and the function of criticism, nor do we have the chance. When these semi-literates succeed in getting out of the clutches of the freshman English instructors, they pretend that they do not like English or think it a useless subject and hasten into commerce or into some so-called practical subject in which they think literacy will be less in demand. I do not have to make good with anybody, and I tell you as fellow citizens that the situation in our American schools is desperate. Boards of education are too often ignorant and neglectful, parent-teacher associations are absorbed in trivialities and social ends, and parents are uninformed and helpless. Superintendents and principals are too often incompetent and indolent, and, instead of doing their jobs, hide their incompetence behind a screen of fancy methodology. Let us hope for their own sakes that after this war the rest of the world will escape from the spread of the American school system, unless that system can learn to operate with greater thoroughness in the teaching of fundamentals.

But fortunately there are good schools and good parents and there is a remnant large enough to save Israel. We may well and must perforce devote ourselves to it.

Let us consider more specifically the contribution which we wish this lecture to make to the general idea of the course. As an example of imaginative integration and by way of further introduction, let us consider briefly the present task of colleges and other institutions engaged in the instruction of men entering the armed forces. My illustration has to do with the doctrine of human liberty. When Plato visited Syracuse he offended Dionysius by his free criticism of the government and was in consequence turned over to Pollio to be sold as a slave. The ground of his offense was his contention that states should be governed by laws and not by men. This principle has been in the world ever since and in one form or another has manifested itself many times in human government—perhaps most often and most consistently among Anglo-Saxon races. I should like to see this principle now identified, amplified, and traced down to our own day, for I think it is the essence of our tradition of freedom and personal liberty. I should like to see added to it by way of amplification Milton's doctrine of liberty; for Milton, as all the world knows, presented a philosophy of liberty, which he regarded as a beneficent, generative force. The thought that liberty tends to create all the virtues—

and his idea, though long neglected, is worthy of credence—has never been refuted and has a very real bearing on our true motive in fighting the present war. John Locke is as important to Americans as to Englishmen, and the doctrine of liberty under the law, which we believe in, found a convincing expression in his writings. The tradition of liberty came to Jefferson strengthened and vocal and lost none of its clarity in the minds of Lincoln and Wilson. There are in our history and in the history of our literature thousands of voices which support the principle that political liberty is a creator and sustainer of national virtue. The concept is perhaps the most important one which could be implanted in the minds of our soldiers and sailors and in the minds of all young Americans who are capable of comprehending it. Its effect would be to make men steady, brave, and resourceful in war and just, honest, and responsible in peace. This is the background of only one idea in a great undertaking, and I offer it as an example of what enlightened thought and imagination may do. Literature is a means by which such ideas may be grasped and felt.

It is, however, my desire to return to fundamentals and to present underlying principles and reasons which should govern our conduct both in war and peace. I wish to show what may follow from the idea I expressed in my first lecture. I suggested there that man's knowledge of mathematics and the laboratory sciences, of the social sciences as such, and of the humanities differs in kind and degree of finality, since what is called "proof" is possible only in the first field mentioned, higher degrees of probability in the field of the social sciences, and lower degrees of probability in the all-important field of the humanities. I pointed out that man must nevertheless proceed in his projects of living in spite of the fact that the most intimate and necessary part of his environment offers the most serious difficulty in its determination, since the process of systematic thought is one and the same, no matter to what end it is directed. I tried to make it clear that man is inescapably involved in all areas of the field. I objected to intellectual isolationism and implied that it is as unwise for the humanist to remain ignorant of the sciences and the social sciences as it is for the scientist to ignore the humanities. In my second lecture I objected to having specialists shake their fingers at us and implied that I thought their specialties, aside from technological language, were rather easy to understand. But, in any case, these three areas of learning are divisions of every man's environment whether he wishes it or not.

Now the struggle of man with his environment results in a synthesis which may be described as man's personality or individuality or character, and this struggle with his environment is a battle in which he has to engage irrespective of his intellectual capacity, his vitality, and his ambition. It may even be said that man inherits an urge toward the mastery of his environment. The great certainties of life, as G. G. Atkins says (*Reinspecting Victorian Religion*, p. 79), are never reached save through the entire ripening of life toward the unseen and the eternal.

A student might well say to one who has just said this, "I haven't the least idea how to make 'syntheses,' as you call them. I am willing to do my part, but I do not know how to make syntheses." The odd thing about it is that nobody knows how to make them, for the good and sufficient reason that they make themselves naturally within the human mind. Nature has said to the student, "If you will read and understand all about, let us say, literature—its content, the men who produced it, the times in which they lived, the bases of their opinions, their inspiration, and sympathetically their feelings—I will make you a cultivated person in the field of literature. You will be a protractor of what is called civilization. You do not have to worry. It is my job to educate people and to make syntheses, and it is your job to work earnestly and sincerely."

Carlyle held and stated repeatedly a doctrine of originality which concerns us immediately in this connection. In "The Hero as Priest" in *Heroes and Hero Worship* he says, "Absolutely without originality there is no man," and in "The Hero as Man of Letters" he says that to be true to the origin of things is originality. The fundamental characteristics of Carlyle's hero are this originality plus a complete sincerity. "The merit of originality," he says, "is not morality; it is sincerity." In a fine passage in the former lecture Carlyle says:

The believing man is the original man; whatever he believes, he believes for himself, not for another. Whole ages, what we call ages of Faith, are original; all men in them, or most of the men in them, sincere. These are the great and fruitful ages: every worker, in all spheres, is a worker, not on semblance, but on substance; every work issues in a result: the general sum of such work is great: for all of it, as genuine, tends toward one goal; all of it is additive, none of it subtractive.

From this doctrine of individuality, an inevitable difference in every man supported by complete sincerity, there follows a remarkable deduction and one worthy of careful consideration: the discovery of truth is originality.   In the fields of science and scholarship no one would call this in question.   Also in a consideration of great writers, like Milton and Shakespeare, and their works I think few would deny the validity of the proposition, for the enduring achievement of these men is the discovery of truth about man's life and about man's relation to his environment. But one must entertain no fragmentary conception of truth.   One must, for example, be willing to admit that perfection of representation is a part of truth.   One must see that truth includes fact, process, form, aspect, and significance.   If it is contended that the characteristic of great art is creation, it may quickly be admitted and may be reconciled with our hypothesis by pointing out that the primordial aspect of God or divinity is not only creation but redemption.   When a work of art approaches adequacy, it is creative of course, but it also is redemptive, restorative, and interpretative.   There is no segregation of factors; the whole tends to the discovery and the revelation of truth.   Art is an affair of the individual and not of the manipulation of materials.   Every man is to some degree an artist, and art and its discovery of truth are natural.   They are often matters of simplicity and tend to associate themselves with naïveté.   The very words "science" and "art" promote pigeonholing or thinking in terms of words rather than in terms of things, relations, and actualities.

Let us return to the urge for conquest and adaptation which characterizes the mental life.   Again we find in the book quoted above (p. 96) a suggestive expression of the idea:

> We grow into ultimate realities and reach our strangely different fruitions because we have thrown the creative force of our dreams, our needs, our idealisms toward dimly seen realities in which we believe we shall find our peace.   We search a proper soil with all the questing roots of our being, or lift our higher growth toward a light and atmosphere proper to our needs.

The author adds, "In a vaster and far more subtle way, life is a kind of quest for responses, and we find them after our seeking."   Now, if we apply these words, not only to man's quest for God, as the author intended, but also to our aims and purposes as scholars and teachers, we enter a very familiar territory.   We arrive, for one thing, at an approach to higher education.   We have called it the imaginative point of view.

First of all, let us consider the simple quality of imaginative thought in ordinary affairs. The point will be sufficiently clear from an illustration. Some months ago when Prime Minister Churchill was delivering an address in the ruined Guildhall in the City of London, he told about the defeat and destruction of German submarines in the Atlantic and said, "They foundered in the deep, dark sea," thus suggesting the horrors which must be enacted in a submarine which sinks to the bottom of the ocean with live people inside of it. The newspapers which I read printed "floundered" instead of "foundered," and the imaginative penumbra was lost. It is obvious that imagination in simple non-structural matters is largely a matter of penumbral suggestiveness. Read these three little poems and see what they are worth without their background of human life and experience:

We be three poor mariners,
Newly come from the seas;
We spend our lives in jeopardy,
While others live at ease.

And will a' not come again?
And will a' not come again?
  No, no, he is dead,
  Go to thy death-bed,
He will never come again.

Even such is time, that takes in trust
  Our youth, our joys, our all we have,
And pays us but with earth and dust;
  Who in the dark and silent grave,
When we have wandered all our ways,
Shuts up the story of our days.
But from this earth, this grave, this dust,
My God shall raise me up, I trust!

Now it is evident that any background, whether of fact, opinion, experience or feeling, to be of any significance, has to take life while it gives life. How it does so is a mystery of the imagination. A famous Greek archeologist, whose special interest was the sculptured groups in the pediments of the Parthenon in Athens, describes how he sought for a long time among numerous fragments of ancient works of art which lay scattered about the building. He was looking for the lower part of the body of a certain statue whose upper part had long ago been carried into the museum. There was one seemingly shapeless stone, a mere lump, lying in plain sight at a point where many people passed and re-passed. They sat on it sometimes or used it as a footrest. Ultimately the archeologist's search brought him to that stone. He examined it doubtfully and finally tried it out. It fitted the other fragment and proved to be the lost part of a statue by Pheidias. It added beauty and meaning to the upper part, and in itself took on both significance and beauty. What I should like to know, and I think the answer will tell us something about the nature and function of vitalized background, is: What happened to that shapeless block of marble thus to transform it and bring it to such abundant life?

I am interested in a quite general application of the imaginative principle. Can we achieve imaginatively a greater faith in education, both in the validity of what we teach and in the possibility of teaching it? Or we might put the question in another form: Can we approach our life work in such a way that we and our pupils may realize the larger background significances of living? If a barber thought of himself, not as a mere tradesman, but as one who may make his fellow men cleaner and handsomer, he might be a better, happier, and more proficient worker. If those who sell groceries thought of themselves as purveyors of wholesome food at honest prices, in other words, if they realized the actual significance of their service, it would be a better service. If those who conduct restaurants knew that they are the hosts of the modern world and that within their dining rooms companionship and conviviality, in the root meanings of these words, might brighten the dark and worried lives of men, they might grow in self-respect and responsibility as public servants. Finally, if our services of combat and their numerous auxiliary forces realize how the future of the world depends upon them, will they not work and fight, and it may be die, in the greatest contentment possible in such a task?

In a larger consideration imagination thrills me with the spectacle of what has happened to man on this planet. When I contemplate the eons of time when the igneous rocks were formed and the pattern of earth was taking shape, it seems to me that the earth must have been meant for life and ultimately for intelligent life. I am at least pragmatically right, since the earth has served and is serving these purposes. The earth for long periods was idle and empty, and, when life at length appeared on earth, it presented a puzzling, a long-enduring, and, as a whole, a tragic picture, full of cruelty and of purposeless waste. There were strange growths of every sort in the ancient ages of the earth. There were mighty saurians and savage beasts, "all teeth and belly and claws, wallowing in fetid swamps, and gorging themselves on other living things. . . . This kind of ghastly shambles, without a gleam of intelligence or a trace of gentleness" went on for myriads of years (G. A. Studdert-Kennedy, *I Believe*, pp. 40-45). The world seemed to be a "ghastly joke" perpetuated by a stupid and indifferent torturer. But into this world there came eventually a gleam of intelligence. Our ancestors, the primates, developed hands and the skills of mind that go with hands. Then began the slow conquest of force by intelligence, so that our ancestors eventually invented houses, families, wheels, books, pictures, and machines. Even so, we were not at the end of the road. Man learned other things even stronger than intellect. He learned wisdom and apprehended causes, mercy entered his heart, and beauty visited his being. If these tendencies are truly determined, and I think they are, who is he that will set bounds to the growth of man? God must have had a primal necessity in his being to have employed such a long, slow, cruel sequence of trial and error; but, however the question may be resolved, we are forced to give God his time. We may even believe in beneficent purposes and even believe that the best times lie ahead.

From our more limited point of view we may therefore say that the gist of the matter seems to be found in the individual man, that his history on earth indicates that this is so, and that his social welfare lies ultimately in enlightened freedom. We believe that man's cardinal action lies in the discovery and acceptance of truth and that he has a natural bent toward this enterprise. We believe that the imaginative apprehension of ultimate truth is his best hope for earthly salvation and is the realization of his being. We would present these considerations as guides and stays in the education of all men.

CHAPTER IV

OPPORTUNITIES IN HUMANISTIC STUDY

In the book of Proverbs, for instance, Wisdom is introduced as
frequenting the most public places of resort, and as rejected when
she offers herself as the natural appointed guide of human life.
"How long," speaking to those who are passing through it, "how
long, ye simple ones, will ye love folly; and the scorners of delight
in their scorning, and fools hate knowledge? Turn ye at my reproof.
Behold I will pour out my Spirit upon you, I will make known my
words unto you."

IN MY LAST lecture I tried to develop what I thought of rather
vaguely as the imaginative point of view in the study of literature. I had in mind what James calls "the perception of
essence," or, as Locke called it, "sagacity," and I thought that
this imaginative point of view would put the mind of the literary
student into "the state in which it will be most fitted to observe,
or most likely to invent." (See *The Principles of Psychology*
[1904], vol. II, pp. 330-31, 340-71 *et passim*.) I saw that only
a sufficiently extensive and accurate knowledge of literature could
enable and inspire the student to reason effectively about literature and its relation to life. Literature would thus, I thought,
become an instrument, both effective and available, in the education of youth.

I based what I said on faith in the value of a diversified experience in all the field of learning. I recognized also the utility
of trained attention and perception in the development of memory
and imagination, and I showed that I knew of no road to these
ends except the beaten path of industry and effort. I made something of a hero of discrimination, and I expect to go still further
in that direction, for discrimination, or the ability to see into a
situation, is basal to selection, and selection, in turn, to the ability
to identify and dissociate essential features. We might thus arrive
at greater and more habitual proficiency in association by similarity, or the recognition of likeness among percepts and concepts.
There is, of course, plenty of association going on always in human
minds, but much of it is local, temporary, and unimportant.
Among the uneducated and the untrained it is merely association
by contiguity, the mind being tied to and hedged about by the

[42]

incidents and routines of daily life. If it is true, as Bain and James taught in the psychology of a generation ago, that association by similarity is to an extreme degree the basis of genius, its development is an end in education. It represents, in point of fact, the improvement education seeks to bring about in the behavior of minds, for, with all its blundering forgetfulness, education strives to develop and encourage this more selective kind of association in its study of art, literature, science, and practical affairs.

An ideal of the maximum possible sagacity should be before each individual student, an ideal which may be roughly described as that of being or becoming something, rather than an ideal of doing something. It is equally important for teachers, and neither students nor teachers can proceed very far on the road unless they can somehow arrive, slowly and gradually it may be, at this conception as a pattern of action. This ideal may be presented on many levels, and my present purpose is to show the opportunities for the exercise of sagacity, or the quest for truth, in the field of literary study. It is my belief that, beyond routine essentials, we may in practice, even in advanced study, learn to do by doing, and that we may be trained and inspired by the perception of problems in the pursuit of truth; indeed, that we may assemble our equipment and remedy our defects in the presence of tasks undertaken. One may or may not recognize the importance of solving problems which arise beyond the scope of one's own present interests and experience. In the field of education the student, until he is able to criticize it intelligently, is wont to follow the lead of learned men, nor is there any objection to this practice, provided that the student ultimately comes to occupy an original position toward the subject and its problems.

I would begin with what Bacon calls "the pleasure and delight of learning"—that almost unaccountable thing which has picked you and me out of a generation given over to the pursuit of practical affairs and placed us in the halls and classrooms of universities. Bacon says:

Again, for the pleasure and delight of knowledge and learning, it far surpasseth all other in nature: for shall the pleasures of the affections so exceed the senses, as much as the desire of victory exceedeth a song or a dinner; and must not, of consequence, the pleasures of the intellect or understanding exceed the pleasures of the affections? We see in all other pleasures there is satiety, and after they be used, their verdure departeth; which showeth well that they be but deceits of pleasure and not pleasures: and that it was the novelty which pleased and not the quality; and therefore we see that voluptuous men turn friars, and ambitious princes turn melancholy. But of knowledge there is no satiety, but satisfaction and appetite are perpetually interchangeable; and therefore appeareth to be good in itself simply, without fallacy or accident. Neither is that pleasure of small efficacy and contentment to the mind of man which the poet Lucretius describeth elegantly,

Suave mari magno, turbantibus aequora ventis, etc.

It is a view of delight, saith he, to stand or walk upon the shore side, and to see a ship tossed with tempest upon the sea; to be in a fortified tower and see two battles join upon a plain; but it is a pleasure incomparable, for the mind of man to be settled, landed and fortified in the certainty of truth; and from thence to descry and behold the errors, perturbations, labours, and wanderings up and down of other men.

But your modesty will perhaps tell you that there is nothing more left to be discovered. Bacon saw this also and gave an answer:

Another error . . . is a distrust that anything should be now to be found out, which the world should have missed and passed over so long time; as if the same objection should be made to time, that Lucian maketh to Jupiter and other heathen gods; of which he wondereth that they begot so many children of old time. and begot none in his time; and asketh whether they were become septuagenary, or whether the law *Papia*, made against old men's marriages, had restrained them. So it seemeth men doubt lest time is become past children and generation; wherein, contrariwise, we see commonly the levity and inconstancy of men's judgments, which, till a matter be done, wonder that it can be done; and as soon as it is done, wonder again that it was no sooner done: as we see in the expedition of Alexander into Asia, which at first was prejudged as a vast and impossible enterprise; and yet afterwards it pleaseth Livy to make no more of it than this: *Nil aliud quam bene ausus vana contemnere*; and the same happened to Columbus in the western navigation. But in intellectual matters it is much more common; as may be seen in most of the propositions in Euclid; which till they be demonstrate, they seem strange to our assent; but being demonstrate, our mind accepteth them by a kind of relation (as the lawyers speak), as if we had known them before.

Modern science, social as well as physical, has only made a fair beginning. In point of fact the number of men who give themselves wholeheartedly to research is not and never has been very great. Most scholars, although they discharge a useful function in society, devote themselves to rearranging, restating, and reassembling the already known. There is great need of scholars who devote themselves to the discovery of new truth. They are the men in the first line, and there arises the question before every young scholar whether he shall be in the front line or in the service of supply, which I take it is in this case usually the education of the young.

In the spring and summer of 1938 I was engaged in seeking manuscripts of Elizabethan translations of Machiavelli's *The Prince* and manuscripts which had bearings on such translations. The consequence was that I read or examined many English manuscripts dating from the sixteenth century. I worked mainly at the British Museum and the Bodleian Library, but not exclusively so. I was impressed with the enormous amount of possibly important material in the fields of school learning, history, the history of religion, and the history of literature which lay there apparently unknown and unread, and this, not only in the great bodies of more recently collected manuscripts, but also in the older collections, like the Harley, the Sloane, the Lansdowne, and the Digby. Some of these manuscripts seemed not to have been read by a scholar since the days of John Strype, and the whole spectacle seemed to me to be at once an indictment of our scholarship and an invitation to future generations of scholars.

Not only are there new fields undreamed of or only vaguely apprehended, but the older fields are filled with error which is sadly in need of eradication. Hundreds of statements and traditions from older scholarship are wrong or wrongly based or in need of verification. This is particularly true of the social sciences, and of language and literature. History and criticism need to be continually rewritten; for each age sees itself as in a mirror. Each age is able to make its own contribution to truth. Repetition, conservatism, and originality characterize the process, and there is a gradual approximation to unalterable truth. It is actually possible now to know and understand Shakespeare better than ever before by virtue of the fact that he has passed through the minds of Dryden, Theobald, Johnson, Malone, Coleridge, the nineteenth-century German Shakespeareans, the New Shakespeare Society group, Dowden, Bradley, Poel, Chambers, McKerrow, Greg, and Dover Wilson. I am sure this aggregative feature characterizes also the history of many branches of the natural sciences. Only careful training and the adoption of a research point of view will enable scholars to set our present field of learning in order. It is primarily a matter of the point of view. Most of the great interstitial or borderline territories between the various disciplines, as that between history and law or history and ethics, have been but little exploited.

Many disciplines have been forgotten and need to be revived. There are lost opinions as well as lost arts.

There remains always the gigantic task of interpretation or re-interpretation, necessary for the health of learning and the welfare of civilization and needing to be done over again in each generation. Only those minds directed steadily to the search for truth can perform this function.

The question that confronts every prospective scholar, every graduate student, is, "Shall I make of myself an original force?" This force may be great or small, important or unimportant, but it is our goal, our opportunity to realize our powers to the uttermost possible extent.

Let me quote, by way at once of summary and addition, a paragraph from *The Lost Radiance of the Christian Religion* (1924) by Principal L. P. Jacks of Manchester College, Oxford:

> The Dean of St. Paul's [W. R. Inge] has recently stated that the problem of human government still remains unsolved. It remains unsolved because in and by itself it is insoluble. It becomes soluble only when placed in strict subordination to other questions that are far more vital than itself. Treat man, after the mind of Christ, as a being whose first need is for light, and whose second need is for government, and you will find that as his need for light is progressively satisfied, his need for government will progressively diminish. This is the only solution of the problem of government. Reverse the order, treat him as primarily a subject, whether of God, or king, or demos, and what happens? The politics of the world will tend toward chaos, as they are now doing, while religion will decline step by step until it becomes indistinguishable from moral pedagogy, whose impotence has been demonstrated by innumerable failures. The struggle for power has now involved the whole fabric of our civilization, and each new phase of it leaves the final solution more remote and unattainable. It is the inevitable consequence of reverting to the idea of *domination*, as the key of God's relation to man and of man's relation to his fellows. On that ground the doom of mankind is perpetual strife. There is nothing for it but to fight it out, and to go on fighting it out, phase after phase, till civilization has spent its resources and the higher energies of the race are exhausted.

In this paragraph is an expression of the immediate and pressing need our world has of a *rationale* for the adaptation of intellectual behavior to a situation which seems to be at its point of crisis. I think the church is trying to point a way out for the world. I think the agencies of higher learning are also aware of the issues and are making efforts to meet them. I see no reason why, at such a time, they should not unite more closely in their efforts, and I think that the differences, both in principles and methods, between religion and higher education will not be found to be so very great.

So far as I am concerned, I have been trying to say, humbly and unpretentiously, that I see at least a hope in a higher, more responsible, and more widely disseminated intelligence. I am a university teacher, and I can talk only in terms of my trade. I see the problem inevitably in terms of the responsibilities of universities and colleges, although I am aware of the responsibility of every other group or institution which has something at stake in our society or an interest in the perpetuation of order and the redemption of civilization. Our basis of procedure in institutions of higher learning is what we call scholarship, and by scholarship we mean no narrow thing but the whole expanse in which the minds of men have devoted themselves to the search for truth. My hope is that this scholarship, this search for truth, may attain greater values than it ever has before and in fields which, because of their difficulties, it has neglected. Can it tell us how we may attain wisdom, justice, courage, and fortitude? In order that you may assess with me the likelihood of any hope which we may place in even a greater scholarship, let us examine frankly and simply the aims of scholarship as we have known it and some of the activities of scholars. These things for obvious reasons I shall draw largely from my own field.

In the reign of King Joash the Books of the Law, which had been lost for seventy years, were rediscovered, and Judah was at least temporarily restored to the truth. Humanity has a way of losing the books of the law, of losing sight of the truth. This comes about, not always because the law books are actually lost, but often because they are superseded by doctrines that seem better to a current world. To find the truth, whether it is lost in fact or merely in oblivion, is the function of the scholars of the world.

During his lifetime Dr. Frederick James Furnivall, without any wealth of his own, secured the publication of a great mass of material necessary to the understanding of Chaucer, Spenser, Shakespeare, and of the whole formative period of modern English literature. Professor Francis J. Child taught the world to hear the music of Chaucer's poetry and to understand his language, brought into the service of humanity a conception of the beauty and strength of the popular ballad, and showed the social and historical importance of the ancient songs of the people. In the fields of both Chaucer and the ballad he gave the world new, or rather forgotten, sources of delight. Perhaps it would be better to say that he taught the world to exploit these subjects and gave rise to the great schools of learned men who have been our leaders for two generations. He has no exclusive claim to having opened these vast important areas, and our debt to many of his followers is as great as our debt to him; but he stands as a discoverer of the books of the law. The late Professor Frederick Jackson Turner did more than perhaps any other one man to make America known to itself. *The Significance of the Frontier* and his paper on *The Social Forces in American History* are in and for themselves works of great strength and importance, but their significance for us lies in the fact that they have guided the researches and enlarged the appreciation of generations of historians, educationalists, geographers, economists, sociologists, and all thinkers about the United States of America. They have made Americans conscious of themselves and therefore better Americans. In the works themselves and in the opening up of a vast and important field of study and thought, Professor Turner was exercising at its full the social function of the scholar, namely, to discover, or rediscover, the truth, to interpret it, and to show its applicability to the life actually being lived.

There is both a developing and a traditional truth, and both kinds of truth are needed in the world. Both kinds must be kept bright and operative. Man has made certain discoveries about living happily on earth and in society and about making terms with his own nature, and the fact that our generation and the ones immediately preceding it have fostered scholarship by such means as the founding of graduate schools, libraries, and research centers indicates that we in this age, in spite of the din of modernists, still believe, indeed believe more strongly than ever, that the past has something important to teach us. We believe that scholarship can teach us something about what it means to live in society and to appreciate how people have lived and do live together, and thus enable our youth to develop such abilities and ideals as may qualify them to secure the welfare of humanity in a rapidly changing society; in other words, can secure for us what Arnold meant by getting to know "the best which has been thought and said in the world" and then turning upon this knowledge "a stream of fresh and free thought," so that our stock notions and habits may not be rejected outright but only as they deserve to be rejected.

There is thus in the world a profession which might be called the learned profession. Its practitioners are scholars. They are not, though they often prove to be, primarily teachers or men of letters or scientists or publicists. Scholars have a function of their own, and they show even the external markings of a craft. We recognize this when we say that scholars are absent-minded, careless about their dress, laborious, kindly, and generous; also when we say that they are extremely businesslike in the practice of their profession, accurate and incisive in speech, impatient of nonsense, and vigorous if not cantankerous in maintaining their own opinions about matters which, it seems to us, could make very little difference whether decided one way or the other. We have heard echoes of bitter controversies over the number of stresses in the original Germanic poetic line, over the authorship of various and sundry uninteresting minor works of bygone ages, or over small emendations or even the right to emend. To this day controversies arise in our learned journals at the slightest provocation over matters which by any stretch of the imagination cannot be made important or significant.

But we must remember that the profession is very old, and that the professors themselves vary widely in their interests and their abilities. They are, moreover, moulded into a sort of organization according to which they are in honor bound, not only to know what their fellows have done, but to credit to each predecessor his full share of praise and blame. The scholar finds, both in the present and the past, men like-minded with himself. Scholarship is not a solitary indulgence of seclusive and eccentric individuals. A scholar in an American university may at any time find it necessary to enter into the mind of John Tyrwhit, Edmund Malone, or the Reverend Frederick Garde Fleay. He may even enter into a controversy with one of these departed worthies; and, although his adversary happens to be no longer able to answer for himself, scholars everywhere will see to it that the rights of the dead are respected. Again, although the particular tasks of the scholar may seem meticulous and petty to the uninitiated, one must remember the ancient organization of the profession of learning and know that little drops of learning coalesce into bigger drops. These small obstructive points of detailed information get shifted in the elapse of time into patterns of perfect coherence and great beauty. The past is investigable. Chaucer laughs with and at the modern world, and we participate in the funeral of the hero Beowulf on equal terms with his skin-clad followers. The history of civilization since the Italian Renaissance shows that men of learning have been engaged almost as one body in a vast task of enlightenment, not yet completed, whose object is the comprehension and interpretation of the ancient to the modern world. There was, first of all, the age of grammatical interpretation and rediscovery extending from Petrarch to Bentley; secondly, perhaps, the age of criticism extending from the late 17th to the middle of the 19th century; and, finally, to some degree, the age in which we live, which should be, if it is not, the age of re-interpretation and re-discovery. Such scholarship has as its intellectual *raison d'être* in the modern world, not only the restoration of a longer and richer past than ever, but the task of making good the forgetfulness of science and of combatting the inroads of pragmatical modernism, the successes of which are usually partial and often factitious. The need of scholarship remains and grows greater as the world grows older and more complex.

Both the functions and the characteristics of scholars have long been recognized, and it is interesting to check up what has been said by reference to popular conceptions of the typical scholar. The hand of the dyer is subdued unto that in which it works, and the professors of learning no more escape that fate than do the professors of law or the professors of dramatics. Chaucer, for example, gives us in the "Prologue" to *The Canterbury Tales* a kindly picture of the Clerk of Oxenford, and one so shrewd and so discriminating in its features that we may derive much instruction from contemplating it. There are things about it one does not see at first acquaintance. Chaucer indicates the Clerk's absorption in university discipline by saying that he has "gone to logic," as we say that one has "gone to seed," but we may remember that logic in the fourteenth century was a profound and extensive philosophic and theological subject. The Scholar and his horse both are lean, his coat is threadbare, and he is evidently poor in such goods of this world as are usually regarded as wealth, but the Clerk seems to possess a library of twenty books of Aristotle and his philosophy, which was for those days an extensive collection of books. It is perfectly astonishing in the history of learning how many scholars of closely limited means have collected libraries which by modern standards would be worth millions. After all, it was books that the Clerk wanted and not harps and fiddles. One suddenly gets the impression that sympathy is wasted on this man and that he was really getting out of the world exactly what he wanted. One sees besides that he has the quality of incisive earnestness, excellent form, and academic generosity:

> Souninge in moral vertu was his speche;
> And gladly wolde he lerne, and gladly teche.

Browning has depicted in unforgettable terms other aspects of the scholar. His Grammarian in *The Grammarian's Funeral* personifies the long and unselfish labors of scholarship, so arduous to this day that nobody should ever enter the career of scholarship who is not endowed with unusual physical endurance. It is said by the commentators that Browning had in mind a typical scholar of the Italian Renaissance, and that a humorous sense of the disproportion between the labors devoted to scholarship and its results heightens the dead humanist's indomitable trust in the supremacy of the immaterial. But Browning has more than this in mind. He has in mind the principle, the dictum of the late Professor Child: "Do the job in such a way that it will never have to be done again." Browning also has a historical recollection of men like Boccaccio, always poor, always enthusiastic, always creative. In 1345 a great body of the Letters of Cicero was discovered, and Boccaccio's contemporary, the great humanist Petrarch, wrote the first of his letters to dead authors to Cicero to apprize him of the fact of the discovery. Browning remembers men like Niccolò Niccoli, the textual critic who copied with his own hand 800 manuscripts; Poggio, who unearthed the great hoards of Reichenau, Weingarten and St. Gall; Ciriaco, the archeologist of Ancona, who boasted that his purpose was simply "to awake the dead"; Coluccio Salutati, the enthusiastic seeker for and transcriber of ancient manuscripts; Fra Giocondo, the Aldine editor; Beroaldo, the laborious scholar of Rome; and also the princely Bessarion. These men were the predecessors of Bentley, Du Cange, and Bayle. Browning pays tribute to the mighty labors performed and to be performed by the erudite.

In Carlyle's *Sartor Resartus* is the familiar figure of Diogenes Teufelsdröckh, that German prodigy of learning, that Professor der Allerley-Wissenschaft in the University of Weissnichtwo and author of the famous treatise *Die Kleider, ihr Werden und Wirken.* Carlyle takes advantage of a popular notion that scholars are both musty and unintelligible to fire his own shots with more telling effect. But Teufelsdröckh is not unintelligible nor, though Carlyle insists that he is, unsystematic. The Professor has written his aphorisms on scraps of paper, laid away in paper bags, each bag labeled with one of the twelve signs of the zodiac. When the slips are removed from the bags they come forth in marvelous order and lucidity. Teufelsdröckh embodies the philosophic function of scholarship, and Carlyle has certainly recognized that function in making his hero the mouthpiece of one of the greatest pieces of social criticism uttered during the 19th century.

Perhaps Carlyle himself, one of the truest scholars among the historians of his century, meant to suggest in his comical picture of the large and orbital discursiveness of Teufelsdröckh the chief enemy that assails the scholar. The passion of scholars is learning. Truth is often fragmentary and elusive. Scholars are given to procrastination. They are sometimes the victims of perfectionism. They sometimes continue to study and investigate and fail to embody the results of their labors in tangible form. There is a passage in Carlyle's reminiscences which records his own struggle with this demon. Carlyle's next book after *Sartor Resartus* was *The French Revolution*. By March 6, 1835, he had completed the first volume of that work. On that evening John Stuart Mill, to whom he had lent the manuscript, came in distracted to Carlyle's house at Chelsea saying that he had lent the manuscript to Mrs. Taylor, whose servant, mistaking the manuscript for waste-paper, had burnt it to ashes. That servant is now in company among the shades with Warburton's cook who used the manuscripts of Elizabethan plays for "pie bottoms," but fortunately in this case the author was still alive and able to rewrite. This Carlyle with much distress and reluctance slowly did. It was during the ordeal of rewriting this lost volume of *The French Revolution* that Carlyle had the experience he records in the *Reminiscences*. It is like the story of the spider and Robert Bruce. From his study window he saw a brick mason at work, "the dusty trowel running to and fro and flashing in the light like a swallow." From this vision Carlyle came to the conclusion "that striving after perfection beyond a certain degree was simply foolish." He saw that the man of learning must be content to do certain and honest workmanship up to the limits of his ability, but that the work must go on. It was to him the steady laying of brick upon brick.

We see that popularly as well as historically the scholar is a man of energy and industry and that only a concentrated quality of idealism will make him stick to his job. His job yields so little in immediate glory and emolument that he must usually be a man indifferent to what are called worldly considerations. The scholar has been usually a teacher and not infrequently the philosopher of his age, for he is in position to acquire the point of view of the ages. The true scholar is also a critic both of himself and of others, sternly self-critical and valiant in his upholding of standards. One recalls the labors of Erasmus as well as his wisdom, the valiancy of Justus Joseph Scaliger and of Richard Bentley, the generosity of Casaubon, Camden and Cardan, the philosophic temperament of Jowett and Child, and above all the kindliness of men like Furnivall, Firth, Manly, Kittredge, and Turner. One sees the undying curiosity of the scholar in thousands of men, great and small, who have built up our civilization by building up our youth.

Perhaps the greatest thing scholars may do is a sort of miracle of the resurrection of the dead. Surely there are no reasons why the claims of the dead should not be recognized if those claims are valid. The scholar may hear voices which have been long silent or have grown indistinct through ignorance. He may teach others to hear these voices, and the voices so heard may be salutary or sweet or both. No aspect of scholarship is more gracious than this revisiting the dead. Nothing is better for the race, since it consolidates our gains. In the infinite variety of human talent there are many voices worth listening to. At first only scholars hear them, but later many men learn to listen in. The world makes new friends and has wisdom added to its own wisdom.

As to the future, one may say that our civilization is still most imperfectly known. The mass of men are still in need of this knowledge, and the betterment of our institutions depends on their getting it. The past is not outworn. It is mainly merely forgotten or never comprehended. In this we find what is perhaps the greatest task of the future for scholars. They must interpret the past in the light of our own better science. They must interpret our own better science in the light of the past, for science itself is painfully subject to oblivion. Investigation of the newest science of today is the scholarship of tomorrow. In the second place, scholarship is faced at this time with the task of presiding at a re-adjustment of values, ethical and economic. It is safe to say that without scholarship this adjustment, already overdue, can never be achieved. There is, finally, the perdurable task of discovery and re-discovery, for every race, for every generation, for every new situation.

If future generations are to have that high regard for the achievements of the human mind which is necessary to the existence of civilization and progress, the community must believe that the past has in it something worth having to be retrieved and preserved. The community must have a certain reverence for learning and a desire to see the truth restored wherever it is to be found. It is not enough to have trained individuals and investigators. If science and true learning are worth anything, they will make the lives of all men better and happier. A large body of influential citizens must be vitally interested in the growth and conservation of human learning, for all true scholarship is about life. Scholarship concerns all mankind. All Americans of any degree of culture are deeply concerned with its activities, past, present, and future.

It is plain from what has been said that scholarship has been the agency of progress. Whether in present circumstances it will be able to increase the intensity and improve the application of its power I am unable to say.

CHAPTER V

METHODS OF OPERATION

Nature does in no wise qualify us wholly, much less at once, for this mature state of life. Even maturity of understanding and bodily strength are not only arrived to gradually, but are also very much owing to the continued exercise of our powers of body and mind from infancy. But if we suppose a person brought into the world with both these in maturity, as far as this is conceivable, he would plainly at first be as unqualified for the human life of mature age, as an idiot.

THE EARLIEST example of the systematic teaching of the history of English literature that I have found in American universities was by Professor Henry H. Reed at the University of Pennsylvania in the 1850's, although the public lectures of Coleridge, Hazlitt, Carlyle, and others as well as Warton's *History of English Poetry* had already established the point of view. The historical approach became and has continued to be the principal one employed in America, Germany, and England, not only for teaching, but for research and criticism. The aesthetic point of view of Pater and others in the later nineteenth century became popular in America, and we still see reflected in the curricula of American universities the methods both of the history of literature and of aesthetics. The former is still far more widely employed. The German philological method, now rather fundamentally revised, has always prevailed with us in linguistic study. The use of English composition as a scholastic discipline was begun formally at Harvard in the late nineteenth century and has spread everywhere throughout our schools and colleges.

English departments have lately been much reviled for holding to the idea that books are best read as they were produced in strict chronological order rather than in formal categories or as a means of pursuing special subjects. The criticism has also been directed against graduate study, which is prevailingly historical in method. The historical method may of course ultimately give way to the aesthetic approach, but it seems, I think, unlikely for two reasons. The aesthetic approach has not been neglected in American universities anywhere for more than a generation. Professor Bliss Perry, for example, whose pupil I am proud to account myself, has been a great leader and a magnificent expositor in the field of teaching literature as literature. Teachers of English and directors of literary research have long recognized and employed the principles of the fine arts in the teaching of both literature and composition. The question with teachers of literature is not one of choice between forms and literary figures, of whether the historical method shall be superseded by the aesthetic method or the development of positive techniques from literary teaching, but of whether they shall be permitted to go forward using all available means for arriving at actual and therefore vital and inspiring truth.

Another objection to a complete reliance on ideological literary categories lies with the shifting and impermanent nature of categories themselves. Plato was a great category maker, and the world owes much of its culture to him; and yet his literary categories and those of Aristotle, though no doubt perfect enough in the Greek world in which they lived, are not, magnificently general as they are, adequate to the nature of things literary. Category makers since their time are always only partly successful. What thoughtful man who knows literature can be satisfied with the classification of the Elizabethan drama advanced cautiously by Professor Schelling and positively by Professor Eckhardt? Or who can fail to see that the modern American category of the short-story, based ultimately on the critical clarity of Poe, is at best a makeshift? Literature reflects all life and thought and it must not be put into a Procrustean bed. The presentation of literature solely in terms of types and forms uncontrolled by a knowledge of incessant variation, although useful, even indispensable, is not in conformity with the nature of things, because it is ultimately too narrow. The mind can think only in terms of abstracts, and forms are necessary to thought, but let us not worship forms or teach others that forms comprehend or can comprehend everything and for all time. Operations in terms of forms are merely higher analyses, even when they seek to achieve wide sweeps of combination, as aimed at, for example, in the four-course plan at Princeton and in the School of the Humanities at Stanford. Such admirable plans are mainly super-analyses, although they may offer a welcome opportunity for the partial recording of syntheses. So far as I can see, there is no complete synthesis except that which occurs naturally within the human mind, the thing we call genius or character or personality. Formal teaching may produce that result, let us hope that it does, for it is our only method of achieving our aim; but let us not base it fallaciously on the belief that literature, the record of the human mind, is primordially divided into poetry and prose; that prose discourse must be classifiable into exposition, description, narration, and argumentation; that poetry has to fit into one of the Horatian classes; that all these forms are inevitably divisible into stated, minor subdivisions; that any groups of forms in any field are forever mutually exclusive; or that we have yet solved all problems, even such fundamental ones as the relation of form to content and to emotional and intellectual appeal. I think therefore that scholars should keep their minds open and seek light from every possible source. There is something banal, I may say in bad form, about this business of banning any one approach to literature. Who are these petty persons who wish to dictate to real scholars how they shall proceed in the baffling enterprise of discovering and exploiting truth? I think we had better continue to adhere to the catholicity of true scholarship and true science.

I believe with all my heart in accomplishment through thought; but I do not want the field narrowed, the method conventionalized, or the product standardized. I believe also in the acceptance of self with all its often painful limitations, in the acceptance of self for the purpose of being oneself and occupying an original relation, however humble, to the universe, and I distrust panaceas and formal methods in determining the relation of training to accomplishment. I dislike the mistaking of partial truth for full truth, which is a kind of fallacy, and I call attention to the fact that it may be immoral. I can be more moving with some writers when I say that fallacious thinking may be not only immoral, but the basis of bad taste. I doubt if there is a perfectly applicable general methodology of teaching or of learning to write poetry or stage plays. This does not mean that such methodology as we know should not be used, but only that it should not be worshiped.

There is no small degree of dissatisfaction with current methods in use in the pursuit of humanistic ends. I have no disposition to defend them, certainly not to argue their complete adequacy; but I do mildly resent implications that we who work in the humanities do not know what we are doing and why we are doing it. Mr. Waldo G. Leland in his address before the First Annual Conference held by the Stanford School of Humanities (*The Humanities Look Ahead*, Stanford University, 1943, pp. 57-69) spoke not unkindly of humanistic studies and those who pursue them, but there was implied reproach in his quotations of adverse criticisms from various persons who, whatever their social or executive import- ance, are not in position to know much about the subject. One of them says that what the humanities can contribute to national life should be reappraised. Back of this lies the legitimate, but from the humanistic point of view rather elementary question, *Cui bono?* Another says that one reason why the humanities are threatened by after-war adjustment, which seems to me itself a scarcely warranted assumption, is that American scholarship has lacked "magnetism, creativeness, and a confident objective." This seems to mean that American humanistic scholarship has not devoted itself exclusively to the writer's objectives. I am sure his objectives have not been lost sight of.

There is, however, more in it than this. There is a custom in some quarters of seeking to narrow the field by deprecating formal and technical scholarship. Perhaps it sometimes comes about that some man who has not been successful in the graduate school, who has disliked Anglo-Saxon, or been made uncomfortable by dull or severe teachers, has vowed a lifelong antipathy to technical scholarship and offers substitutes usually drawn from the field itself. Far be it from me to justify dullness and formality or to believe that any human institution will ever be without them. But we are not all that dull and that technical. Such revolution- aries as I have described are sometimes joined by administrators, often bred up in the sciences or the social sciences, who decide *ex cathedra* what the aim and method of the humanities ought to be. Such men often think that we should devote ourselves and our efforts to the creation and exploitation of the gentle and beautiful aspects of life as revealed in art and literature, that we should beautify their practical lives, as if that were possible! We have a subject with a content and bearings, and we too have the right to make our students work that they may understand the significance of their lives, who they are and what they are doing. The men I have referred to above call on us for complete knowledge of our fields and related fields and of all history and philosophy. We usually receive their indictments with a *peccavi;* yet, in Heaven's name, how can anybody know adequately any- thing without long and intensive study, a study and effort which will result in the effectual knowledge and the trained judgment we humanists are expected to possess? We are entitled to be judged by our successes as well as our failures, and it is not our fault that the world is filled with incomplete products, persons who have stopped halfway and have not carried their disciplines through to mastery. Let it at least be remembered that we stand historically and in principle for liberality, for live-and-let-live, and have always had our weapons turned against those who think, because they have made some progress in the mastery of science, social science, technology, or practical affairs, whether administrative or financial, that they know everything and are as gods upon the earth (*op. cit.*, p. 124).

The *locus classicus* of this hostility to scholarship is the late Frederic Harrison's *Among My Books*. "That word of ill-omen known as Research," says he, "hangs upon literature like the microbe of Sleeping Sickness." He hastens, however, to say, "No one who knows me will suggest that I disparage thorough and exact knowledge or show any mercy as a critic to superficial work." And in the same book he points to many authors and ages demanding investigation; specifically, he pleads for a more systematic study of Byzantine history and civilization, a field neglected by English scholars, where "much remains to be done to redress the ignorance of ages, multiplied from of old by clerical bigotry, race insolence, and the unscrupulous avarice of trade."

Most scholars think that research and "systematic study" with such an aim as that—"to redress the ignorance of ages"—are one and the same thing. If they are not, research means something which Harrison thinks trivial, pedantic, and supererogatory. Perhaps he does not want literature subjected to systematic study or research—except Byzantine literature, Homeric literature, Greek tragedy, and other literatures in which he is interested. Perhaps all literature should be spared by research as a thing beyond the scope of investigation. But most of us agree with an old report on Promotion of Research before the American Association of College Professors which affirms "the fact that research in all branches of knowledge," including *litterae humaniores*, "is indispensable." "Who will be so bold as to affirm," it says, "that one subject possesses a practical value and another not, however utilitarian the former may seem?"

An explanation of Harrison's position can be found in two circumstances, both significant. In the first place, he is impressed with the frequently vicious and misleading quality of contemporaneous documents—"as shallow, untrue, even mendacious as contemporary gossip." These in historical study he often sees misused by stupid and prejudiced people. When such documents are scrutinized by "the sagacious historian of a larger purview," he is gratified. His quarrel is with the ignorant and superficial student, whose work is misleading and false, or stupid, like that of a philologist who does not know what philology is about. But there is a second way of handling contemporaneous documents which Harrison finds even more annoying. That is to publish them all without discrimination or interpretation, so that "every scrap of documentary evidence has to be not only seen by the author, but thrust upon the reader."

No man [he says] has any right to make public his thoughts upon any subject until he has thoroughly exhausted and assimilated all that can be reasonably learned about it. But he has got to give us his *thoughts*, not his materials; what is worth knowing, not what can be stated and printed; what conclusion can be reached by Research, not what Research can unearth and cast up in a rubbish-heap. Books are too often made nowadays by laborious poking into charnel houses and dustbins of the past, instead of intelligent understanding of men and things. The first thing and the last thing in a real book is Thought. Tons of Research will not weigh down an ounce of Mind. For this canonisation of dead Facts is the ruin of healthy and pleasant reading. And if reading gives no enduring pleasure it serves no humane purpose.

Most of Harrison's charges are true, and lamentable; yet it is worth while to inquire into the extent and causes of these faults. Harrison demands, on the part of the scholar, long, careful and arduous study resulting ultimately in mastery, and in ability to think and write. In the experiences of each scholar there must be many stages of completeness in these processes. One man will be far along the road to mastery; another hardly more than a beginner, knowing only a little field and not knowing it well. It is also evident that many books are necessary for a scholar's use, that those dwelling near great libraries have an advantage, in the acquisition of mastery, over those who visit well stocked libraries only occasionally. Leisure is required to become a scholar, and those who work for their living as teachers may have little time to perfect their knowledge. American scholarship in English is certainly open to the charge that it frequently lacks form and the maturity of thought of which Harrison speaks. It is also true that American scholarship is fragmentary. It publishes many bits of research, which, taken by themselves, seem unintelligible and unimportant. This practice arises in some measure from the conditions in which the majority of American scholars work.

The English scholar has usually a subject of special interest, and his learned article is usually a fragment of the main structure. He works at Milton or Spenser or Dryden, and the most he is able to do is the minute study of a small part of his field. If one reads the article, one may conclude that the writer is a small-minded person who thinks that the facts and ideas he has got together into a paper for a learned journal are of great importance; but if you look deeper, you will often find that he is a man of vision. He sees himself some day, when books and leisure are more abundant, author of a great work, *the* great work, on his chosen subject, a real book in which the first thing and the last thing is thought. Perhaps his fragmentary publication ought to be discouraged; but looking at it from his end there has seemed to me something rather fine in it—the courage and perseverance of a man who refuses to be beaten in his fight to be a scholar, who defies his circumstances. He will keep alive his humanistic interest in spite of difficulties. In content, form, and intelligence his work will be found much better than could be expected, not inferior, save in length, to certain recent unabridged studies of literary men, and mere length is not a basis for judgment. Is it not, therefore, ungracious for scholars with leisure, means of publication and large libraries at their disposal, to demand respectful consideration for their quartos while they rail at other less fortunate scholars for their small articles?

Our present danger lies, not so much in the direction that Harrison points out, as in the other direction. He himself admits the necessity of work so honest that it will result in intellectual comprehension. We, in our dread of meticulous scholarship, often prefer to devote ourselves to immediate ends and so forget the necessity of curing our ignorance by hard work. This was illustrated by the activities of a committee for the promotion of Renaissance study which met a few years ago under very good auspices. Instead, however, of facing the long, laborious, and difficult task of building up American Renaissance scholarship, they characteristically preferred publication to study and contented themselves with issuing a series of their own hasty articles, and with that let the matter drop.

The whole matter is larger than any question of special groups or special circumstances. It concerns an aim in life. Let us take for an expression of the ideal a paragraph from the late Professor John M. Manly's memorial notice of Professor Francis Barton Gummere in *Modern Philology*, September, 1919:

> Since his death—as often before—I have asked myself what was the secret of his power. He had learning, he had vigor, he had charm, he had—in a measure given to few of his generation—that indefinable possession we call culture; but these qualities, separately or together, hardly account for the total effect of the man and his work. He had the mind of a scientist and the temperament of an artist; or perhaps I had better say he had the mind and temperament of the great artist, the creative imagination which sees its vision as a whole but does not rest content till it sees each detail as a perfect part of a perfect whole. He began his work at a period when the large conceptions of the romanticists in philogogy were just coming under the reshaping influence of Darwin and his followers—a time as rich in ideas and in enthusiasms as the period of the Renaissance. Men who in another age would have created statues and epic poems were smitten with a vision of opening and reading the furled scroll of prehistoric life, of recreating the pageant of civilization from its remotest beginnings, of painting their half of the picture of the origin and destiny of man. It was this creative vision, this vitalizing imagination, which gave its charm, its power, its unity to all that Professor Gummere spoke or wrote. Literature was not for him a heap of dead leaves shaken from the tree but a living part of the body of life. He knew this and he made others share his knowledge.

The output of American scholarship in English is no doubt disappointing, but it is not a closed issue and a formal thing. What the doctors of philosophy have published, contrary to the opinions expressed by critics, is possibly better in proportion than the work of more mature scholars. When English scholars have given themselves two or three years of comparative leisure in some institution with a proper library, they have written books of some merit; whereas, after they have entered the treadmill of college teaching with its ever increasing burden of instruction and administration, they find less adequate expression.

Some writers complain that when the scholar has turned to creative literature, he has felt the deadening effect of his past discipline on his imagination, wit, and style. It is doubtful if this is true generally. The probabilities are that the persons in question, like many of us, have never learned the art of literary expression. "Studies teach not their own use," says Bacon, "but this is a wisdom without them, and above them, won by observation."

A far more general complaint is that scholars who are drawn towards literary creation are constantly repelled by the general university attitude towards scientific method, and the fact that the latter is rewarded and the former is not; also that scholarly activity is enforced instead of voluntary. Theirs is surely a different world from the one I have lived in. The men who have won reputation, salary, and influence most quickly in my acquaintance have been, first of all, those who possessed what is called administrative ability; secondly, those who produced original literature. Such literary men are regarded with pride by their colleagues, by the authorities of the university, and by the alumni. They are the envy of other institutions. I have seen but little compulsion of any kind and, on the other hand, have been deeply aware that ability and industry are much needed in American colleges and universities and are usually recognized.

Certain methods of scholarly approach have also been objected to, but there ought to be no improper narrowing of the field. The nature of the subject will vary with the individual, the equipment, and with the thought impulse of the times. It is said, for example, that the study of sources is a foolish and useless thing. No doubt source hunting has been carried to a ridiculous extreme and often done in a stupid way, but it ought not to be forgotten that this method of study has yielded a great deal and is neither a contemptible nor an unphilosophic method of approach. Originality and imitation subsist side by side in the same individual, and the human mind must always draw its materials from outside itself. The original man will be original even when he tries to imitate, and superficial originality may be the basest of imitation. There is often more imitation of the obnoxious kind in a current bestseller, with its new plot and its banal ideas, than in whole blocks of word for word copying by Ben Jonson, Sir Walter Scott, or William Shakespeare. Sources, for one thing, enable students to grasp the ideas that influenced great authors and thus to understand them better, even to appreciate the play of their geniuses.

If critical persons choose to narrow their definitions of scholarship even to a point where it excludes its traditional and most obvious activity, it does not greatly matter except locally, and, if they are quite successful in their revolt, they themselves may at some future day become the subjects of fruitful, judicious, scholarly investigation; or, if administrators so misconceive the nature of universities that they discredit or cast out scholarship in certain fields, there will still be much for their faculties to do, and university administrators are not immortal. Nobody with a grain of sense doubts that scholarship is an instrument of power and effectiveness in the education of the young and the continued education of the old.

We declare our independence of credits and degrees and have said we want the real thing. We have refuted those who wish to narrow the field of our action and have declared our intention of studying literature in any way that we want to, for we think that literature is a great cultural instrument. Let us now in conclusion present, by way of illustration of our point of view, an example of the application of learning to literature. We shall talk about the contemporary treatment of ancient themes.

I once examined the scholarly, as distinguished from the more strictly critical, reactions to a certain popular book which came out a number of years ago, and I think the report may serve to render concrete some of the general things I have been saying about the point of view of scholarship. I think it will make clear the problem continually presented in the teaching of the literature of the past.

With reference to every piece of ancient literature studied or read there are roughly two points of view. There is the point of view of the age which produced the work, and the point of view of the age which reads the work. This is a commonplace of criticism, yet nevertheless it is not so widely and accurately observed in practice as its obviousness would seem to necessitate. The ordinary reader appears with his ordinary equipment. He finds in the work of literature just such qualities as he is able to appreciate, and the others he lets go unknown or misunderstands. This is the general, the almost universal method. It results no doubt in the conservation of important ideas from age to age, and, in so far as art is universal in its appeal, it keeps alive artistic pleasure from age to age and maintains an artistic tradition. Perhaps the body of critical literature may be said to rest on this basis. With reference to a particular work of art, criticism would ask whether or not it is so fundamental in its appeal that man as man, in his most basal relations with his fellows and in his most intimate problems of the conduct of life, cannot cease to understand and appreciate it.

The most striking example that can be cited in illustration of ancient themes so treated through the ages is that of the Homeric poems. These poems have apparently lived on and let anachronistic criticism or interpretation do its worst for three thousand years. Their longevity is largely because the situations which they present are still recurrent. We have not outlived our ability to understand them or to be moved by them. In spite of the feeling of being completely new which comes to each generation, and with particular force to certain generations, we may believe that *Iliad* and *Odyssey* will continue to have their appeal for thousands of years to come. I have tried to account for this, and have found a doctrine of ultimate social stability, which may, perhaps, be the merest commonplace.

However much the intelligentsia of any age may change their religious and philosophic points of view, there seem to remain relatively untouched in human life certain fundamental relations, partly philosophic, partly biological, partly social, partly economic. Even when outposts are stormed and taken, even when daring forays have advanced to the walls of the citadel, the main body seems still in a position to laugh a siege to scorn. However much repressed or discouraged, the body of human instincts remains intact. Wandering and acquiring, mating and maternity, fighting and resenting, flight, subjection, and hiding, parental, filial, and gregarious instincts, along with imitativeness, curiosity, and communicativeness, show no signs of diminution and only minor signs of change. A like permanency seems to belong to egotism and altruism, to courage and cowardice, self-respect and degradation. Men are still subject to health and disease. They still live in the world and breathe its air and do well or ill merely as living creatures, and sustain and feel and reflect on the effects of existence. How can it be otherwise? Men are still poor or rich, bond or free, commanding or subordinate, subject to loss and bereavement, burning under oppression or towering in the point of pride.

Now, it is this immutable body of conditions, or if not immutable, changing but slowly, with which the Homeric poems so largely deal. Literally hundreds of illustrations can be drawn from the pages of *Iliad* and *Odyssey*. Widows are common enough and pitiable enough still in this world which has so much to say about the failures and faults of the marriage relation. But let us hear Hector as he bids farewell to Andromache and foresees her widowhood after his own impending death in battle:

> Yet doth the anguish of the Trojans hereafter not so much trouble me, neither Hekabe's own, neither king Priam's, neither my brethren's, the many and brave that shall fall in dust before their foemen, as doth thine anguish in the day when some mailclad Achaian shall lead thee weeping and rob thee

of the light of freedom. So shalt thou abide in Argos and ply the loom at another woman's bidding, and bear water from the fount Messeis or Hypereia, being grievously entreated, and sore constraint shall be laid upon thee. And then shall one say that beholdeth thee weep: "This is the wife of Hector, that was foremost in battle of the horse-taming Trojans when men fought about ⌐ Ilios." Thus shall one say hereafter, and fresh grief shall be thine for lack of such a husband as thou hadst to ward off the day of thraldom. But me in death shall the heaped-up earth be covering, ere I hear thy crying and thy carrying into captivity.

You will think of the battle over the body of Patroklos and see Achilles go forth to battle clad in his marvelous new armor with irresistible passion burning in his heart. And later godlike Priam will go to the tent of the son of Peleus, and clasp his knees and ask for the body of Hector, his son; and you may remember him in some occurrence in daily life. That great personal and domestic story *Odyssey* is almost fuller than *Iliad* of enduring human situations.

Iliad and *Odyssey* will take care of themselves as they have always done. Men will read them as they have always read them, and understand of them only so much as they can translate into terms of current daily life. All this is well enough; but during the last three quarters of a century, and now and then before that, another element has come into the criticism of the Homeric poems. This has been brought in by scholars. Life in the Homeric age has been studied by archeologists and philologists, and certain scholars whose genius it was to exercise the historical imagination have said, "Wait; you have read Homer, but do you know exactly what it was that Homer meant to say. Because of the lapse of time, change in custom, change in man himself, much that Homer meant to say is now obscured. Read with my eyes and I will show you new beauties. I will teach you, if you will cease your narrow credulities long enough to learn it, to penetrate this hidden secret by means of your own imagination." It would be absurd to deny that this scholarly type of criticism has met with success. So much so that when an American writer chose to treat a Homeric theme in what I have indicated as the traditional manner; namely, with wilful disregard of the principle of the historical imagination, he was assailed by some of the leading scholars of the world. I refer to Professor John Erskine and his *The Private Life of Helen of Troy.*

Let us take up this theme of Helen of Troy by way of illustration. Helen first runs away with Paris from the home of her husband Menelaus. Paris takes her to Troy, and the Trojan War ensues. Then, after the fall of Troy, she is received back into the home as the wife of Menelaus. As you will see at once, both of these episodes, her running off with a lover and her being taken back by her husband, are of such a character as to engage the cordial interest of our age in that department which we think of as our morals. Running away from husbands with lovers is the stock in trade of our fiction; and when it comes about that the husband takes the "erring" wife back into his home, we have something in the realm of the extraordinary and the enticing; there is something to be accounted for.

Homer does not exploit either theme, and *Iliad* and *Odyssey* are not consistent with each other. Homeric religion and morals are hard to understand and yield their secret only to sympathetic study. Moral responsibility was largely an affair of the gods. The gods were usually responsible for moral dereliction, but it is not correct to think of this as fatalism. Men were the creatures of the gods and entertained feelings and compunctions for their wicked actions, though the responsibility for these actions was usually placed upon the gods. For example, Helen was ashamed of what she had done and the misery and death she had brought in her wake to Troy, but the responsibility for her conduct belonged to Aphrodite, the goddess of love. Then again Helen was the embodiment of beauty, and beauty to the Greeks was all-compelling and irresistible. Let us take the scene from *Iliad* where Helen is in the presence of the Trojan elders:

> These had now ceased from battle for old age, yet were they right good orators, like grasshoppers that in a forest sit upon a tree and utter their lily-like voice; even so sat the elders of the Trojans upon the tower. Now when they saw Helen coming to the tower they softly spake winged words one to the other: "Small blame is it that Trojans and well-greaved Achaians should for such a woman long time suffer hardships; marvelously like is she to the immortal goddesses to look upon. Yet even so, though she be goodly, let her go upon their ships and not stay to vex us and our children after us."
> So said they, and Priam lifted up his voice and called to Helen: "Come hither, dear child, and sit before me, that thou mayest see thy former husband and thy kinsfolk and thy friends. I hold thee not to blame; nay, I hold the gods to blame who brought on me the dolorous war of the Achaians."

So far as *Odyssey* is concerned, there is singularly little, if any, reflection of moral turpitude with reference to Helen's flight from her husband, and no surprise that Menelaus received her back into his home as his wife. The implication seems to be that she was a prize worth fighting for and that she had been fought for and won. Menelaus seems well satisfied to possess eternal beauty as his spouse. There is no trace of disgrace. When Telemachus visits the Spartan court, he finds Helen the honored and gracious wife of his host. She is the dispenser of gifts from her rich store. When Telemachus departs we read,

And Helen stood by the coffers wherein were her robes of curious needlework which she herself had wrought. Then Helen, the fair lady, lifted one and brought it out, the widest and most beautifully embroidered of all, and it shone like a star and lay far beneath the rest.

Helen of the fair face came up with the robe in her hands, and spake, "Lo! I too give thee this gift, dear child, a memorial of the hands of Helen, for thy bride to wear upon the day of thy desire, even of thy marriage. But meanwhile let it lie with thy mother in her chamber. And may joy go with thee to thy well-builded house and to thy country."

And thus, as Andrew Lang says, "The handiwork of the cause of all sorrow, is regarded as a fit present for a stainless bride."

Later writers, both Greek and barbarian, have been by no means satisfied to let the matter rest with Homer. They too have felt the desire to read into these situations the psychology of their times, and to eke out by tradition or invention the scanty details provided. The long article on Helen of Troy in Roscher's *Ausführliches Lexikon der griechischen und römischen Mythologie* will show you the numerous additions and divagations which classical antiquity made to the story. Helen was worshiped as a goddess in Therapnae and pictured in the fields of Elysium in the company of her husband. The question of why Menelaus took her back as his wife was also answered. According to Pausanias there was represented on the chest of Cypselus "Menelaus with a sword in his hand rushing on to kill Helen—evidently at the sacking of Troy." And a vase shows Aphrodite rescuing Helen by removing a veil from her face, so that Menelaus might spare her for her beauty. Then again Stesichorus, or a scholiast quoting Stesichorus, tells how the army of the Greeks proposed to stone Helen to death, but when they beheld her beauty, they cast down their stones upon the ground. Vergil did not like Helen and spoke of her unkindly, but she found a defender in a fourth-century Greek poet, Quintus Smyrnaeus, who told her story so well that the earlier and simpler Greek conception of irresistible beauty made its way into the Middle Ages and colored, in the main not falsely, the conceptions of the romance writers. And it is this conception reinforced which flames out in the famous passage of glorious verse in Marlowe's *Dr. Faustus:*

> Was this the face that launch'd a thousand ships,
> And burnt the topless towers of Ilium?

So that, in the case of Helen of Troy, it may be roughly said that scholarship reinforced tradition. You feel this when she is glanced at by Swinburne here and there, as in that matchless vision of the childhood of Helen and Clytemnaestra in *Atalanta in Calydon* quoted by Andrew Lang. It was left, however, for Lang himself to write the great work of penetrative and imaginative restoration in his *Helen of Troy*. When I was a Greek student, *Helen of Troy* was the favorite poem of my friends and me. The modern student of Greek knows it and admires it as he does almost no other modern poem. I think this poem contributed no small amount to the fervor of indignation which found utterance by certain cultivated English critics in presence of *The Private Life of Helen of Troy*, which they could not but regard as a crude and banal performance, if not a desecration.

American critics made haste in the pages of our modernistic journals and reviews to vindicate the author's right to lay hands upon the legend of Helen of Troy; for, said they, there is nothing sacred about it. Helen was to them no sacred figure which might not be besmirched, and the scholarly protest was untimely and unwise, because it was sure to fall upon deaf ears. I have myself begun by justifying the author in saying that he has done a traditional thing. Through him the current school of American sex-fiction insisted on expressing itself through this medium, however much some scholars might loathe the record after it had been made. The time was no doubt ripe, and the book celebrated our complete ignorance of Greek. But after all, what are these ancient stories of Helen of Troy, Lancelot and Guinevere, Anthony and Cleopatra, except media through which succeeding ages may express their particular conceptions of certain fundamental relations in life?

The general method of the book under consideration is a process of rationalizing. The idea of rationalizing and travestying this theme may have come from Philip Moeller's *Helena's Husband*, a playlet published about 1916, although it may have come from older writers who had been the source of Moeller's idea. Use was made of the now familiar device, for whose introduction into literature Mr. Bernard Shaw (e.g., in *Caesar and Cleopatra*) is largely responsible, of shocking those who entertain romantic and conventional ideas about institutions, themes, and situations. What Shaw has to say is pretty widely current. He wishes to tell us that frankness is to be preferred to propriety, that sin is a spiritual matter and not a matter of action, and finally that the denial of impulse and desire, of any character soever, is sin. It, therefore, not infrequently turns out in our modern plays and novels that the open and convicted sinner is the only virtuous and moral person in an entire group of the clamorously respectable. There is nothing unusual in the insistent exploitation of the possibilities of pruriency for which the stories dealt with offer considerable opportunity. It is really fairer to criticize *The Private Life of Helen of Troy* for its rather uninteresting prose and its insistent repetition of the by no means numerous propagandist principles which seem to offer the moving and propelling principle of the work.

One simply throws the whole matter of anachronism to the winds; one condones or forgives the desecration of a theme precious to lovers of Greek literature and tradition, and the best that can be done is to account for Menelaus' re-acceptance of Helen on the ground that he is a coward and a weakling. One forgets the dark-bearded giant who fought the duel with Alexandros on the plains of Troy. Menelaus is merely Babbitt, who has an astonishingly enlightened, patient, frank and fearless wife, who unfortunately loses much of her charm because she talks too much. Menelaus has besides, what is not at all unexpected, an extraordinarily priggish daughter, a thing which may happen to anybody at any time; a gate-keeper of surprising wisdom and modernistic insight, or shall we rather say that one of those proficient butlers of the then current English comedy had taken service as gate-keeper under Menelaus of Sparta. Such and such like are the anachronisms of *The Private Life of Helen of Troy*. I prefer the frank and unconscious anachronism of Shakespeare, but what, after all, is anachronism? A sophisticated modern age has to be anachronistic in a sophisticated way. And the underlying causes that gave us *Troilus and Cressida* and *The Private Life of Helen of Troy* are largely the same.

Scholarship has no propaganda and does not take sides. Its newest and best phase is avoidance of anachronistic thinking on its own part. Its business is to seek for truth, and its temper is undogmatic. In the case just considered it would discriminate among the various versions and significances of the story of Helen of Troy.

CHAPTER VI

THE ACADEMICAL INSTITUTION

It deserves to be considered, whether men are more at liberty, in point of morals, to make themselves miserable without reason, than to make other people so; or dissolutely to neglect their own greater good, for the sake of a present lesser gratification, than they are to neglect the good of others, whom nature has committed to their care.

LET US TAKE our bearings in this course of lectures by reference to the three aspects of the mental life—to know, to feel, and to resolve. In the earlier lectures we placed special emphasis on knowing. We went farther perhaps than would be thought practicable, but we did so for several reasons. There is no doubt that the growth of knowledge in the modern world has been immense, but we argued that the effects of greater actual knowledge have been rather to simplify than to make knowledge more difficult and also that later college generations in America have been starving in the midst of plenty. The knowledge has remained dead and inactive in books and has not come to life in the only way in which knowledge can come to life, namely, by being taken into human heads. I thought also that perhaps our modern specializations were too narrow and that in order to live, even to live the life of the narrowest specialist, in the modern world, our great need is for students to broaden their minds and realize themselves as human beings in the world. I suggested also that we take too lowly a view of the capacity of the brain and that we might be much better specialists and at the same time much happier people and better citizens if we knew more. I had no idea that amassing information as an end in itself was praiseworthy or desirable, but I thought that a better educated youth might give us a basis on which to build American culture on a vaster scale. To direct our efforts toward the early discovery of genius is certainly desirable, but I had in mind, not so much the development of genius, as the cultivation of originality. This I thought of as a property of every man, which Carlyle thought could be revealed only by sincerity. I thought of it also as one and the same with the discovery of truth. I thought it essential for the highest ends in education to attempt to discover the mental processes leading to originality. And yet my aims were simple enough. I thought of the practical aim as the raising of the general level of intelligence among American college and university graduates.

I was one of the original group of preceptors in the educational experiment at Princeton which was known as the Preceptorial System. I was engaged in that experiment for five years, and my opinion, which, although unchecked by the opinions of others, I believe to be true, is that there was a great improvement in the general level of undergraduate scholarship at that place. Whatever battles among the gods may have been raging in the skies over Princeton in the later of those years, candor compels me to say that in my experience I have never known so great a college as that was and such a high degree of intellectual interest and vitality in any undergraduate body. Now the thing that happened was not exactly what one might think. The numbers and proportion of men of the very highest intellectual genius were not greatly increased. *Fortes ante Agamemnona erant.* But what happened was that students of C and D standing almost disappeared, and the students we usually graded A and B absorbed the grade sheets and proportional grading almost broke down. That widespread mental elevation of an undergraduate body has been for me since those days an unrealized ideal, an almost utopian dream. What I now express is an ideal of more vital intellectual life in the American academic world, and my own experience forbids me to say that it is impossible.

My own sincerity and the present situation in which we find ourselves, with the vision of our failures, our present responsibilities, and the impending possibility of both dangers and opportunities, have attended well enough in my lectures to the element of feeling. I at least can speak without thought of personal interest. I have suggested that literature and many other subjects might do their share in bringing about a world in which there would be habitually in the generations always something original, for I thought that literature might seize the imagination or kindle in case after case in unending sequence that inward illumination which comes to the world from the enlightened individual who has learned to express himself and not another. Self and therefore originality are inscrutable, and I have tried to avoid quackery. I have rested my case on simple things like industry, sincerity, and a sense of duty. Can we by the grace and mercy of God make our educational institutions true channels of inspirational forces?

This brings us to the third aspect of our mental conception, which has to do with resolving or with action. Let us therefore consider our subject from the point of view of the academical institution.

The university system inherited from the Middle Ages consisted of a group of small units—halls or colleges—where students and teachers lived together in a pupil and teacher relation. These smaller units were tied together by the university, a formal organization which had to do with matters of common interest to the halls and colleges, such as course of study, the granting of degrees, and the conduct of the exercises by which men qualified for the degrees, exercises which discharged the same function as our examinations do. The university also supervised the conduct of students outside their halls or colleges and maintained the public relations of the university. (Oxford and Cambridge still send representatives to Parliament.) The system I have just described was characteristic of Italy, France, Spain, the Low Countries, and Germany. It has lasted effectively only in England and in some of the colonies.

The organization into colleges and halls, on the one side, and the university, on the other, divided the operations of higher education in a very interesting fashion. The university proceeded by means of formal tests, public lectures, commencements, and the police. The control thus supplied was usually democratic in the sense that the smaller units chose their governors and by means of convocations made or altered university laws. Indeed, except in certain governmentally controlled universities on the continent of Europe and in a good many American state universities, higher education has always been democratic. The university was an official and impersonal institution from the start.

In the halls and colleges, faculty and students lived and ate together. Because in a small society ruffianism and idleness cannot be tolerated, since the offenders are too close to their masters, the colleges and halls now and then resorted to expulsion or rustication and in earlier days to corporal punishment, although in these early days and later their discipline generally took the form of moral suasion. There is a tradition that John Milton was whipped by his tutor at Christ's College, Cambridge. If so, it was an awful spectacle; but it at least may be said that there was no lack of intimacy between Milton and his tutor. In the college there was no indifference, no take-it-or-leave-it attitude. The colleges operated in general very well indeed, built up a community spirit, and were popular, often beloved. From this small college is descended, not only the American small college, but the American university.

There were certain things the colleges could do because of their situation. They could be thorough and could particularize their teaching. They were excellent in inculcating manners and morals. Associations between faculty and students were mutually beneficial and were convenient, since faculty and students were associated in those three great human occupations—eating, sleeping, and loafing. The colleges were thus admirable in the better kinds of mental training, such as the application of learning to life. The students wrote many papers, both formal and informal, and discussed them with each other and with their teachers. Books, although not always abundant, were close at hand. The colleges developed solidarity and group-spirit, which processes are, I take it, extremely educative. Faculty and students became friends, and sometimes no doubt enemies; but they were not indifferent to each other. These things—thoroughness, manners, morals, community spirit, free discussion, friendship, sharpened intellectual outlook—are still within the grasp of the American small college. I do not know to what extent they make use of their advantages. It is a notable fact that leaders of our country in all lines have come in disproportionately large numbers from small colleges. This tendency may be on the wane now. I do not know. Small colleges have often been too poor to maintain their faculties at a high cultural level. Buildings and equipment have often been cheap, poor, lacking in comfort and convenience, and not adapted to the job. They have not always been able to feed and house their students or to meet them for association in the ordinary routine of living. Having students dine in faculty homes is excellent, but at best it is a makeshift. The college is the thing, and it should be the place where the community eats, sleeps, plays, studies, talks, and works. Such association is discipline, and our poverty and ignorance have no doubt caused many colleges to relax their discipline. Remember that it was the university, and not the college, which operated by means of a police force (proctors and bulldogs). Real discipline comes from membership in a properly constituted social institution, and not from compulsion or from organized moral instruction.

A very interesting thing happened to some of the colleges established in America, no less a thing than the invention of the American university. Harvard, Yale, and others were colleges which so outgrew themselves that something had to be done about it. The college became a university. This had happened on the continent, but there institutions surrendered their educational responsibility, and contented themselves mainly with impersonal activities—instruction, examination, the awarding of degrees, and some aspects of public behavior. Their students might study or not as they liked. But in America, when the colleges became universities or when new universities were established outright, they continued to try to exercise the intimate controls belonging to the original small college. They have not been very successful in this matter, the job has been too big, although some very interesting experiments have been made in some universities to restore the traditional academic way of life with its intimacies and responsibilities. Within recent years, particularly in state universities, institutions of higher learning have taken on an organization modeled after private business, in which the faculties have become hired men and the students customers. Princeton made, and I think still is making, a noble effort to be both a college and a university, but the going is hard, and in most places it is given up as a bad job. "Let the dean of men and the dean of women do it," we say, or "Let the committee on examinations and standing throw them out if they do not pass their examinations." The western universities hardly know of anything else and do not know that students have ever been treated in any other way. In the East, they have tried with some success to bridge this fatal gap by means of tutors and residence houses. The problem remains unsolved, and I do not know a perfect solution.

In two other calamitous matters, both arising out of the anomalous nature of American universities, our situation might be bettered. In taking on the ancient university function American universities made a fatal mistake. They left examinations in the hands of the college teachers themselves. College teachers had had to assume an unnatural function because of isolation and necessity, and it was left in their hands. American universities are still floundering in the toils of this octopus, which makes it impossible for the university itself to tell the difference between good teachers and poor teachers, robs college degrees of any ascertainable and certain value, and, worst of all, puts college professors and college students, who ought to be natural friends, in opposition to each other. How can college students be really friendly with a man whose duty it is to label them with an A, or a B, or a C, or an F? And who knows whether his judgment is worth anything or not? Whereas, if examinations were given by an indifferent board, students and professors would become partners, and the whole relation between them would be changed at once, changed, for example, to the attitude that prevails in English colleges.

The other remediable fault arises out of the growing disposition to regard universities as business institutions instead of universities. I resent being regarded as a hired man and prefer to think of myself and my colleagues as persons devoted to the service of our country through the education of the young. We have not such and such an amount of time and instruction to deliver. It is our duty to give all our time and all our brains to our job, and our real reward is in our profession. We are partners in an enterprise, and we are members of an academical body. I think that the learned body should include everybody from the newest freshman to the oldest emeritus professor. Can we not admit to actual membership in the corporate body every student and every faculty man? Can we not open the doors and say to every comer, "This house is yours and this is your family? We are all engaged in one enterprise and we differ only as the members of families differ, some of whom are older and wiser than others."

This same misconception has helped to cause the creation of a vast and wasteful process of what we call administration. Now, some administration is no doubt necessary, but in general it is a thing which we ought to study how to get rid of. There are simple ways of doing these things. One office of record with carefully registered precedents for all action and with all university committees operative at that center, such as they have at Stanford, would save much valuable time. Look at the simple way in which Oxford and its colleges (no small affairs) are run. Let us center our minds on our ancient and perfectly well understood job and avoid as much as we can all this multiplication of correspondence and conference and, above all, these educational gadgets. There are some bad features in our academical institutions, but we all know how to do our work, and things might no doubt be worse. They are worse in some large institutions where the faculties have lost control over educational matters. "Power corrupts," wrote Pascal, "and absolute power corrupts absolutely," and some universities are ruled by autocrats who are not so much interested in maintaining faculty enthusiasm and efficiency as in publicity, riches, and a good front. This state of things is not very widespread as yet, but it is important that American higher education should return, not only to democratic principles, but to faith in democracy. This is in order that we may regain control of our institutions, which have more and more been taken over by the students and are devoting themselves to athletics, to social ends, and to irresponsible materialism.

I should like our universities to reassume their proper functions and stop the tendency to serve merely as matrimonial agencies and as asylums for youth in the dangerous period of late adolescence. I remember some years after the first world war, when I was being locally pestered by a theory of speeding up the educational process, that I overheard at tea at King's College on the Strand some men talking about the writings of M. Pierre Janet, a noted French psychiatrist. I was interested by what they said, and I read a number of Janet's publications. One of them was based on an examination of some ten thousand cases and seemed to show that most mental aberrations and social misfits come about in late adolescence between the ages of seventeen and twenty-two. I saw that the idea that a man ought to take his bachelor's degree when he was fourteen, his master's degree when he was fifteen, his Ph.D. when he was seventeen, and become a statesman when he was twenty-one was badly out of joint biologically. I saw that people do not grow up until they are grown, and M. Janet said that that time for women was about twenty-one and for men about twenty-two. I saw the harmful absurdity of being in a hurry about this business of higher education. Janet said that it was advisable for youth during the period of later adolescence to live in fairly sheltered conditions where they could try out many things and broaden and deepen their minds and characters with knowledge and thought. It occurred to me that the four-year American college had accidentally hit upon an important group of years and that there was an actual and simple rightness in going through college. Of course I knew that many colleges can serve society only as asylums, and not very good ones, in getting these youngsters out of the way at a time when they are socially obñoxious. But I saw also a new significance and importance in college and university education. I saw the vast need for guidance in education of untold thousands of young people year by year in unending stream, and I saw that the greatest need of society is to have its members started right. I saw that the primary service of colleges and universities is to furnish society with better citizens and that that was practically the only service which universities could properly undertake for their undergraduate students. What I learned seemed to indicate that specialization ought to come later. Now colleges and universities are places where bad habits, such as idleness, vice, and antisociality, may be fixed upon a man; and I do not see how we can sit apathetically back and let students run wild or herd themselves under their own often trivial and ignorant leadership.

This conception of the virtue of breadth in education brings me back to my more special theme. I hope that I have reinforced it by an authoritative suggestion worth further consideration. I do not think the conditions in which we work are in every way advantageous, but I do not regard them as irremediable. Many of them can be, and let us hope will be, improved, and American youth are still naturally ambitious. I believe that the study of literature in our colleges and universities is at this time a saving grace and that it has further possibilities. University students need the intimacy of association which it breeds, the community of ideas which it establishes, the union of man with his fellow men which it brings about, and the vision of beauty, truth, and goodness which it lifts up, like the bronze serpent in the wilderness, before the mind.

If we assume a liberal point of view and if we endorse, as I presume most of us do, the double function of the academician, discovery of truth and its propagation—or, as we say, research and teaching—there are some simple matters in our situation which require explanation and attention. If both these functions are recognized, they are both worthy of reward and they should both be taken into consideration. The hired-man conception of college and university teachers has been holding us back and doing us and our function harm, the idea, namely, that teachers, particularly younger ones, are really not members of the academic body but are hirelings brought in to meet so many sections per week and to read papers until their eyes dazzle. Now that is necessary and fruitful work, and I am no revolutionary. I merely recommend a square deal, for I think that every college teacher is entitled to the privileges appertaining to membership in the academic profession. It should be taken for granted that every college teacher has work to do in the pursuit of learning, and he should have at least some free time for scholarship and administration. I think this is a matter of practical importance.

I think also we should understand that our organization of graduate study provides for two kinds of study, and I think they should be discriminated. Graduate schools offer advanced courses, very desirable and often necessary. They should be well presented and followed up industriously, for they are often a liberal education in themselves. But graduate courses are not all to be described merely as harder courses than are undergraduate courses. There are also research courses, and the characteristic of genuine graduate study is research. It follows that students graduate into genuine graduate study, and if there is no research, there is no graduate study. Research courses, of which there are fewer than one would think, do not need to be numerous, but such courses do need to enter basically into the training of every young scholar who is launching himself in his career.

What we need to heed is the caution given in the Epistle to James (i. 23, 24), "If any be a hearer of the word, and not a doer, he is like unto a man beholding his natural face in a glass: For he beholdeth himself, and goeth his way, and straightway forgetteth what manner of man he was." The mind learns and retains only that to which it pays attention, that which costs it effort. The untrained mind never learns anything except that in which it has a private interest. It is perhaps not too severe a thing to say, that we have a piecemeal system of education—so many courses each term, so many credits, such and such total number of credits, resulting in a degree. Now a degree may or may not be evidence of an educated mind. Our students often leave us with practically no memories. They have had a lot of important and interesting stuff put before them and they have very often responded to it at the time, but each bit they have put away without use or subsequent resort. They are like the man in Jeremiah's parable (xiii. 1-11) who hid the girdle in the hole in the rock, and when he came to look for it, he had to say, "Lo! it is marred."

In the foregoing description of our present American academical institutions I have showed a disposition to complain, I hope not querulously, that present institutions are not functioning as well as they ought to or perhaps as well as they could. If you in this university are entirely satisfied with advanced education as carried on here, I hope there is solid ground for it, and I congratulate you. In that case, I am merely talking about large and less favored regions, and you will join sympathetically with me out of a patriotic interest in the welfare of higher education in our country as a whole. I feel that there is a great unsolved problem in American higher education, and I justify myself for bringing it forward on the ground that its factors, even its existence, its bearings, and the baneful perplexities which arise out of its unsolved state, are neither widely understood nor realized in their significance. Dissatisfaction has been expressing itself very widely in terms of its attack on this or that academic subject and in mutual recriminations between departments or in attempts, such as my own, to bring about harmony among the sciences, the social sciences, and the humanities, or between general and specialized study. In point of fact, these debates are only superficial and the roots of the problem lie far deeper. The problem itself is simple, and I should like to suggest it by the quotation of a short paragraph from an article of which I shall proceed later to make greater use. I refer to an article in the *Atlantic Monthly* (Vol. cxxix, 1927, pp. 153-66) entitled "Hardscrabble Hellas," by Lucien Price.

> We have seen what this school could do without money. Now what can it do *with* it?
> This question is a good deal larger than Hardcastle Academy, and that is why it is raised. It is a question which stares out of countenance pretty much the whole of American education. The heathen thought they should be heard for much speaking. Our institutions of learning appear to think they shall be heard for their much brick and bullion. Yet the question is even larger than this. It is as large as the machine civilization of the Western world. Those Connecticut pioneers founding their school in an oak forest are type and symbol of the age and race that sired us. When we were young and poor, our poverty and struggle bred men. We grow prosperous. And now what are we? This wealth—is it to be a bed of care or an alpenstock? These machines—are we to use them or be used by them? I have likened Hardcastle Academy to Periclean Athens. Both perished. But both lived on. Both failed. Yet both triumphed. And these United States? Are we to be yet one more gluttonous and grasping Rome, physically powerful but spiritually sterile? Or is another Athens to rise? Shall the world's great age begin anew, the golden years return?

This is the author's comment on a change of conditions which has occurred in the United States mainly since the beginning of the twentieth century. Many of us are old enough to remember the days of relative academic poverty. No doubt hard conditions still exist in less opulent regions of our own country—in the South or elsewhere. We all bear testimony to the effect that the poorer institutions of those days were educationally better than the richer institutions of today. We are all getting older, and perhaps we are deluded by the familiar fallacy of the "good old times"; but I do not think so. I think, with every desire to be candid, that we have lost or are losing some things essential to our educational effort. Now, what are those things? What did the students of my generation and older generations get that present-day university students usually do not get? I should like to suggest two things which I think are fundamental. First, students were required to know something exactly; they had no choice in this matter. Secondly, they had, also without their own volition, an opportunity of coming into contact with men of inspiring personalities, these personalities being directed rather habitually to an intellectual approach. Not all college and university teachers were of such a kind, but there were enough and they were available. Indeed, man for man, I think our current university faculties are superior in culture to the men of the earlier time and not inferior in teaching skill and moral earnestness. But the conditions of those days enabled college teachers to exercise greater and more immediate influence than our conditions permit or provide for. It is not merely the fact that we teachers are swamped by numbers. If it were, that could in time be remedied. Our better facilities ought to be and could be made advantageous. In some places a great deal has been done to facilitate and encourage study. I think Parrington Hall at this place is an instance. Laboratory sciences maintain close contact between teachers and pupils. The case is not hopeless, but the fact remains that many pupils in our greater units, both high schools and colleges, are without discipline and are not obliged to know anything exactly, indeed, avoid knowing anything exactly and are able to escape by means of the soft spots in our curriculum into idleness, ignorance, and excessive social activity. Their numbers being what they are, they sway the public voice of the student body and of the community, so that education in the university is minimized, and it is commonly believed that students go to college in order to meet people, make friends, and secure social advantages. These things are available and have always been, but to make them ends in themselves is to ruin the university as a national cultural force. We have teachers of excellent training and ability, more books, and better quarters, but our students are not obliged to pay any attention to us and in some places have lost faith in us. How can we restore that faith? How can we make our academical institutions function more effectively? Dr. Woodrow Wilson said to me, "These students are too busy with their own social affairs to pay any attention to you. If you hired a window on Wall Street and accosted one of the stock brokers rushing by and said 'Hold on there! I want to tell you something about a poet named Chaucer,' he would say, 'I have no time to listen to that stuff. I'm earning a living.' And when you say the same thing to one of these students, he reacts in exactly the same way and says he is making a club." Nevertheless in those very conditions the preceptorial system did make a remarkable impression. It did so by requiring students to know their subjects with some exactitude and by providing them, not only with the opportunity, but with the necessity of coming into contact with men of mature intellectuality.

The article I referred to above is the story of a poverty-stricken academy in a small Mid-Western town, where, in spite of hardships, it wrought the miracle of transforming youth, so that youth thus transformed might transform the world. It was no very gentle and polite place. It was harried by hazing, ravaged by homesickness, and blown upon by the coldest of cold winds. "If," says the author, "the windy plains of Troy were much windier than these bedrooms on a January night, Helen showed poor judgment in ever leaving home." He says that the sons of farmers and country-town professional men took the rigors in their stride, and announces some almost forgotten principles in saying that physical hardships appeal to youth. He actually dares to say, "What a stupid superstition it is that boys naturally detest study. What they do detest is a bore. Youth is the hero-worshiping age. Give me a hero schoolmaster and I will guarantee that the intellectual passion gets kindled in any mind that is combustible." He tells about one hero schoolmaster in whose classes there was a sport "as definite as football practice" in which his game was to stick the boys, and their game was not to get stuck. The author goes on to show the breadth and liberality of the cultural scope of that poor little place—in the classics, in modern literature, in creative writing, in all studies. I have known such institutions myself, and I should stultify my own thinking if I did not say that in some of those poor fresh-water colleges I have seen an intellectual life more vigorous than I have ever seen in great and rich universities. I like summer school teaching, and I have gone back to the State University of Iowa summer after summer for the sake of finding people to teach who really wish to learn.

I do not despair of what may be done about this in universities, but my attitude is militant. We are no doubt greatly successful in many cases, but I think we are failing with reference to the job as a whole. We have lost our disciplinary power, and I do not see how we can succeed without it. As soon as any teachers or departments put the screws on, their enrollment rapidly decreases. The students find out easy professors and easy departments. I want it distinctly understood that I do not make my attack from the point of view of the subject studied. Any subject in the curriculum can be made to yield its full cultural value if it is taught in the right way. The ordinary faculty man is powerless, but the administration is not so, and I know of no service half so valuable which an administration might render as to go through the institution and see to it that, as far as possible, the mean advantage of the snap course and the easy degree are done away with. It is usually not necessary to fire a lot of people but only to make a few new allocations and to appeal to personal and professional pride.

Let us not make a mystery of simple things. All the world knows the job, and it is unnecessary and harmful to surround it with a blur of methodology and technical language. We all agree with John Milton in the *Tractate on Education* when he said that a completely educated man was one able to perform with justice, skill, and nobleness of soul all his duties, "both private and public, of peace and war." American education made a rather bad showing in both the great wars, and our educational services in these emergencies would have been more effective if our educational institutions had done better what they were supposed to be doing anyhow. As my colleague Professor E. W. Knight says ("Education in War and in Peace," *North Carolina Education*, January, 1943), "Few of them [educational institutions] had the courage to hold to the view that a sound educational program need not have to adjourn its legitimate and constant activities in emergencies, whether economic or military." And he adds, "Apparently we forgot that real patriotism, in war or peace, is intelligent, purposeful, and effective citizenship, and that schools that do not develop in people the capacity as well as the disposition to serve the best interests of the country, in peace as well as in war, are obviously defective." Like Professor Knight I favor no radical revision. I desire that we should strive to do better what we are supposed to do anyhow, and, as I see it, it is not merely a matter of striving. It is also a matter of being given the opportunity to strive. When I remember that in many places freshman English is the only course required of every student in the university, I think that freshman English should engage the best minds that the department has or can find in the whole country and that the course should be made so fundamental, so inspiring, and so stringent that to take it and pass it would be at once a guarantee against illiteracy in our graduates and a ticket of admission to all the courses in the university which require and expect hard study.

The suggestion I have just made is so threatening to our comfort and so laborious and disturbing to the university numerically and as a whole that I feel like withdrawing it at once. The truth of the matter is that all teachers of freshmen and sophomores ought to operate in that way and I believe that, under proper leadership, they could be induced to do so. Such a policy would do much for the enormous burden of remedial labor laid upon us. We are now faced with the maxim, "Too little and too late." When I and my department at the State University of Iowa were engaged in a struggle to prevent illiterate persons from getting degrees, Dr. Walter A. Jessup, then president of the University, said to me not unsympathetically, "You are eight or ten years too late; what you are trying to do ought to have been done in the grades." And he meant in all the grades. I have always held that the situation is bound in course of time to find a remedy, although the remedy appears but slowly. Nevertheless we in English have as our subject our native tongue, a great language, and the literary tradition of our race, a great tradition. A knowledge of our subject is indispensable, both socially and intellectually, to the cultural progress of our fellow citizens. Our subject, among all the subjects in the field of learning, has the power to awaken, to encourage, and to inspire. It has the rare advantage of being needed by men in every field. I have talked about it rather formally, for my purpose has been to place it as honestly as I could in the midst of the American academical institutions.

But this has not expressed my feelings about it. It has not even done justice to my faith in the subject. I hope it has not even suggested that I regard English language and literature as the special property of English teachers, for I regard English, as distinguished from our courses of study, as the property of every man who speaks the tongue and in large measure as the principal force that holds us together as a nation. Nor do I wish to exaggerate the importance of English in institutions of higher learning. English language and literature are the affair of the nursery as well as of the university. Great literature appears in *Mother Goose*, and I can prove it. Where can you find more beautiful and more vital rhythms; more accurate and more expressive words, more completely effective thought than in the childhood jingles of our race?

> For want of a nail a shoe was lost, for want of a shoe a horse was lost; for want of a horse a rider was lost, for want of a rider a kingdom was lost; and all for the loss of a horseshoe nail.

> Solomon Grundy, born on Monday, christened on Tuesday, married on Wednesday, took sick on Thursday, worse on Friday, died on Saturday, buried on Sunday. This was the life of Solomon Grundy.

> Curly locks, curly locks, will you be mine?
> You shall not wash the dishes nor yet feed the swine,
> But sit on a cushion and sew a fine seam,
> And feed upon strawberries, sugar and cream.

Where is there wisdom superior to that of "The Little Red Hen," or ethics superior to that of "The Pig Brother"? I know no greater hero in romance than the Marquis of Carabas in *Puss in Boots*, no story of greater essential pathos than *The Beauty and the Beast*, no villain, not Iago, more threatening than the Yellow Dwarf. The great ballad of *Sir Patrick Spens* is a record of nobility in hardship for the ages, and I well remember the effect upon me of *The Twa Corbies*. Surely, after our population has settled down and become more native to the soil, mothers and fathers will read and sing good literature to their children, and not have them build up their vocabularies and their characters solely from the comic strips. Perhaps they will again read *Jack the Giant-Killer*, *Goody Two-Shoes*, *Tanglewood Tales*, *Pilgrim's Progress*, *Robinson Crusoe*, *Tom Brown's Schooldays*, and *Alice in Wonderland*. Why not *Ivanhoe*, *Old Curiosity Shop*, and *Little Women*?

Let us quit experimenting with youth while there is still time and not follow the dreadful road taken by Italy and Germany. Let us let youth be young. Let us even insist on their staying young. We cannot change the sequence of the seven ages of man. It is unwise for us to do so if we could. Youth will follow childhood, and manhood will follow youth. We are living all the time and are not preparing to live. There is a good life for childhood, a good life for youth, and a good life for mature men. We murder to dissect, and our innovations are often monstrosities. Let our academical institutions work within the bounds of nature. Let us try for good schools for children, good high schools for early youth, and good colleges for later adolescents. Let us try further to humanize these institutions and adjust them to their proper functions. I have suggested for our colleges and universities greater intellectual vigor and a more complete control of our own activities.

On the whole I am not too well satisfied with the academical institution as a place in which to study the humanities. It proceeds by courses, majors, examinations, theses, and degrees, and inevitably regards the study as a completed part in a preparation for living; whereas, the humanities, by their very nature, should enter continually into life at every period. I found this closing idea so well expressed in a quotation from Benedetto Croce in Professor Benham's chapbook, *Clio and Mr. Croce* (University of Washington Book Store, 1928), that I should like to repeat it here:

Hence I have found by experience and in my own person the falsity of that pedagogic theory which restricts education to the first part of life, the preface of the book, and the truth of the opposite doctrine which conceives the inner life as a perpetual education, and knowledge as the unity of knowing and learning. To know and to have lost the power of learning, to be educated and to be unable still to improve one's education, is to bring one's life to a standstill, and the right name for that is not life but death.

CHAPTER VII

THE FUNCTION OF LITERATURE

> What, in particular, is the account or reason of these things, we must be greatly in the dark, were it only that we know so very little even of our own case. Our present state may possibly be the consequence of somewhat past, which we are wholly ignorant of; as it has a reference to somewhat to come, of which we know scarce any more than is necessary for practice. A system or constitution, in its notion, implies variety: and so complicated an one as this world, very great variety.

THE SUBJECT of this lecture is not so much the function of literature in the ordinary sense as the function of the study of literature in higher education. I do not claim for my lecture any philosophical significance whatever. I attempt no definition of poetry or of literature and have nothing to say about the relation of literature to history, philosophy, or the fine arts. I think of literature as a representative art in time and as, broadly speaking, the record of our race, of its better moments if you like, but without the imposition of any particular set of forms. Form to me on this occasion is merely concept, and I do not consider the artistic aspect of form. I attempt rather to recall and organize my own experience as a teacher of literature and on the basis of that try to determine the cultural effects of literary study. Tragedy has seemed to me to be at once the broadest and most fundamental representation of human life, and I shall devote myself in the first place to the tragic.

The ancient contrast between comedy and tragedy is not a contrast on an equal basis and is therefore not entirely valid. Tragedy is so wide in its scope that it may be said to underlie all event. By plot or story we mean selected event, and tragedy seems to include potentially all event. Comedy from this point of view is only an aspect, and its contrast with tragedy lies, not in event or consequence, but in an emotional coloring which attaches itself to event and consequence. Tragedy is far more broadly comparable to the action and reaction, the rise and fall, the attack and recoil, the growth and decay which seem to characterize the whole physical universe, including man and all his works. It is doubtful if there is such a thing as a comic plot. There are just stories, and tragedy seizes them if it likes. I would not split hairs, but it has seemed to me that comedy borrows criticism for its structural use. It really dramatizes humor, irony, satire, utopia, situation, eccentricity, and burlesque; whereas tragedy dramatizes blocks of existence. Comedy steals certain bits of this stuff of life and sometimes burlesques tragedy itself. But comedy seems to be the merry thief and tragedy the properly constituted owner. I merely rule comedy out as a coordinate dramatic form.

There is a very general disposition on the part of philosophers and wise men to agree with the man of Uz who says that man is born unto trouble, as the sparks fly upward. The battle with environment to which man is born constitutes what Sophus Winther calls the cosmic trap. Even resolute or habitual nonparticipation is at best the assumption of a more or less insignificant cosmic rôle and from a larger point of view is itself a tragedy. In this situation men and women struggle, and we believe that in practice, up to a certain point, wariness, skill, and wisdom may provide us with a series of definite escapes. We believe that it pays to be good fighters and that wisdom has something to add to bravery. On this belief, at which many philosophers snap their fingers, we base our hopes in education. We all know that we cannot certainly provide ourselves and our youth with perpetual escape from the tragic ills of life, but for the wary there exist also other devices besides escape, which we believe are, if not escape, at least victory in defeat.

In our ethics (remember that wisdom is a part of ethics!) we are still Aristotelian. We believe as firmly as the Aristotelians and the Stoics, or as Shakespeare and Bacon in the Renaissance, that the terms of the problem of living are two: first, that man must have the courage to undertake and to do and, secondly, that man's hand must be guided by intelligence, not only while it acts, but after it has ceased to act. We know that man's reason must rule and that he must achieve the calmness which comes with self-knowledge and self-control. He must learn to be indifferent to what Hamlet calls "the event." The struggle to act and to act wisely and to do one's best with some indifference to consequences, is man's most typical struggle in the world; indeed, it is the principal struggle of the race of man against its environment, both now and through the eons of time. Now that man is at last partly civilized, the game becomes, not less interesting, but more interesting. This brave and cheerful submission to the will of an inevitable power is the chief thing which Christianity has taught mankind, and let us not forget that, although it has stressed the aspect of man's essential helplessness and told him not to interfere with the ways of God but to submit himself as an obedient child of God, Christianity has taught with an insistent voice that man must act, must do the works of God as a good and faithful servant.

Now, whether we choose to teach this lesson in terms of religion or in the secular terms of ethics or history or science or art does not greatly matter, for the truth is one and the same throughout. As proponents of truth, if we believe this, we have no choice as to what we shall teach. We must make clear as well as we can the nature of the cosmic trap; as, for example, in the matter of physical health, the dependence of body and mind upon exercise and healthful living. We must, if we are sincere, make clear both the relation of life to activity and the relation of wisdom to happiness. The field, as I have said from the beginning, is indescribably vast, and the needs of men, although war, famine, and pestilence may make them temporarily more poignantly obvious, are universal, incessant, and so common that they attract no attention. Ignorance and folly go laughing and weeping through the world and continue to breed in poverty their characteristic offspring.

The simplest and commonest things in life are notoriously badly done. Cooking is in general unskillful. The army has to begin by teaching boys to walk, and walking is one of the commonest of human acts. Breathing is very badly done, and, when it comes to eating, the spectacle is distressing, both as a spectacle and as a field of choice. We eat the wrong things at the wrong times and in the wrong quantities. Age gorges itself and grows rheumatic and obese on food appropriate only to growing youth. Youth rejects a sane diet and feeds on ice cream cones and coca-cola.

One of the things we do most commonly and do worst is talking. Talking is bad, not only from the point of view of vocalization, articulation, and language, but from the point of view of content. There is very little good talk in the modern world and, what is worse, very little discrimination or appreciation. Swift thought that people could talk much better than they do simply by correcting obvious faults, and he was probably right. Man is prone to cowardice, and it comes about that silent, owl-like people are so trusted that they acquire great reputations for wisdom and stability. When we try to find out what is going on in such people's heads, we discover that usually nothing at all is going on there. They say nothing indiscreet, because they think nothing either discreet or indiscreet. They are the material out of which we make our administrators and statesmen. Nothing serious happens unless they begin to take their own brainlessness seriously, and then it is just too bad. We suspect gaiety and brightness and think that it cannot be safe and virtuous to laugh and be witty. The ideal no doubt is wit plus discretion, but, on the other hand, thought and language are complementary aspects of the same thing. We cannot very well find out what we think unless we talk. But talking is by no means directed thinking, and possibly the worst of all conversational vices is that of pouring out in an unending stream the contents of the associative memory. Have you not seen groups of three young persons walking happily across the campus carrying on a lively conversation on three different subjects, no one of them paying the least attention to what the others are saying? Egotism plays a hero's rôle in conversation. Two women are talking about their infants. If they are friends or decently-mannered persons, one will talk about her infant as long as she can with propriety and then listen to the other talk about her infant as long as she must in order to get another chance to pursue what is to her the more interesting subject. This is a better and more sportsmanlike conversation than the kind one generally hears among men. This consists in an exercise easily described. One man simply tries to prove that his motor car is finer than the other man's motor car, or that his house, or his business, or his acquaintance with famous people, is superior to that of the man with whom he happens to be talking. The simple principle in all this is the one announced by Swift to the effect that your affairs can have no more weight with other men than theirs have with you. Swift has a very suggestive study of the subject of conversation, to which I refer you. I use it merely to illustrate the tentative opinion that we are mostly stupid, blundering, shambling, imperfect animals.

The most familiar mental device by which men seek to orient themselves, to understand their existence, is the figure of a journey. The Bible is full of it. Man is a pilgrim or a sojourner. He passes along life's way to another and a better land or takes the primrose path to the everlasting bonfire. No doubt a journey is the best figure of speech ever invented for the purpose, and to many life will seem to be actually a journey. It has become a necessary means of comprehension, so that it seems no longer an invention but a device for doing business with living, as the Ptolemaic or the Copernican astronomy is a device for doing business with the universe. The idea of progression and panorama is dominant in the memory. Life is very like a moving landscape in our memories, even when it was a quite stationary life. Life has also been thought of as a battle or a river or a task. All of these have merit and utility no doubt, and there are other figures of speech in the poets. Indeed, the general impression of existence is a chief theme of the poets.

But one wonders if it might not be possible to find some convincing figure in which to represent the aspect of life which arises out of our weakness and our fears. To express this aspect the travel figure is simply useless. It is an old, old thought, of course, that the past is something to be studied and profited by and that the future is something to be prepared for, and these things are true, but they are merely fragments of the truth. Nobody tells us of the futility of dwelling upon the past or the future as such or of the danger of so doing. The past is also a quagmire in which men and women get entangled, so that they need salvation, and the future is mainly a daydream or an hallucination which it is dangerous to act upon. Today is the only life and the only field of foresight. It is hardly worth while to recollect the past as such; it is almost useless to anticipate so obscure a thing as the absolute future. The thing that is worth while is to have emerged from the past a good marksman and to stand as a skillful hunter at the gap awaiting the future, for the future is concealed in the thicket until the beaters come, and no one knows what manner of game it will turn out to be; not Nimrod himself.

But, even so, it is misleading to introduce the idea of waiting for something vaguely called the future to happen. Time itself, they tell us, is a function of the present, and there is no difference between sight and foresight and none between insight and prudence. Our life is a continuous process of action and reaction between ourselves and the whole of the world in which we live. This interrelation tends to isolate us and to breed antagonism against the world. It is possible for human beings to converse with one another with their lips and be remote from one another in their hearts. Fear, diffidence, prejudice, and falsehood create chasms between man and man, and the only bridges over those chasms seem to be understanding, sympathy, sincerity, and unselfishness. A man may be at odds with his world or in sympathy with it. He may, for example, be at odds with himself, for in this strange sense he is part of his own environment, or he may be willing to forgive himself, accept himself, and on sternly reasonable terms become friends with himself. So important is this that one of our great duties in the leadership of the young is to teach them to do just this. But in spite of these things, there is in human experience that which creates in us a sense of loneliness in the presence of things unknown. Nature and the world, following nature or being dragged recalcitrantly behind it, present immense operations, confusing, inscrutable, and, if not wantonly cruel, apparently uninterested in us. In society too there is an immense and threatening preoccupation which makes the individual think that he does not matter, that he is alone and uncared for and that his best chance is to grab what he can from the whole.

W. E. Hocking says that in so far as a man or woman persists with this picture of the universe before his eyes, he or she is a lost soul, lacking in both courage and confidence. For such a person life has no meaning beyond what can be snatched by dint of self-assertion. It is very shocking to think that this devil's doctrine has been put forward in our country by certain influential groups as an ideal of public education. As long as men feel in themselves this absence of confidence, this selfish impulse of a blind greed, this ignorance of ultimate significance, this dread of calamity and death, this slavery to chance, this ultimately self-defeating selfishness, they are indeed lost souls. I believe that this for some men is a true picture of worldly life, and I know that no individual man has much power in his hands and that dictatorial moral influence misses the point.

The cosmic trap sometimes becomes a trap of the mind, a figment of the imagination, and it is a mistake to think that such imaginary involvements may not operate as deadfalls. "There is nothing either good or bad, but thinking makes it so," says Hamlet, and we are perhaps warranted on this occasion in inquiring whether definite knowledge and clear thought may not enable many people to escape the snares set by the morbid and deluded mind. The world continually mistakes sophistication for knowledge, and our fluid, sometimes superficial, age has been prone to make this dangerous mistake. Out of casually gathered scraps of psychoanalysis, relativity, economic determinism, and fascistic megalomania, certain vocal persons have made a cosmic trap out of an unwarranted theory that life itself is nothing but a cosmic trap. Man himself with his ordinary life has been regarded as merely a hero in a puppet-show, a creature whose thoughts, acts, and intentions are not his own, but are merely the outcome of forces unknown to him in his self-delusion. As Professor Carl Becker puts it (*Yale Review*, vol. XXXIII, 1944, p. 402), "Lacking certainty and conviction, men sought compensation in diverse ways—in blind submission to the authority of church or state, or in disillusionment and indifference, or in a cheap sophistication, or in a conscious and cultivated cynicism nourished by the half-hearted conviction that since the world is meaningless and man corrupt one may as well get what one can while the getting is good."

I cannot on this occasion make an effort to destroy these cobwebs of modernity, but I think there is a major fallacy in the thinking which has given us this false system. I believe it mistakes the part for the whole. I think it has picked out certain phenomena from the general course of nature and organized them into a system consistent within itself and supported by the circumstance of its consistency. Bacon offers a satisfactory explanation of such a factitious philosophy when he says that agreement within the parts of a system is no proof of the truth of the system as a whole. In other words, nature includes all things and with them the possibility of sophistical reasoning. It may be that a broader knowledge and a more patient enlightenment would save us from the tragic possibilities of a misconceived cosmology, in terms of which we accept the belief that this is a universe devoid of purpose. I resort in my thinking to the noble passage in *Areopagitica* which contains these lines:

He that can apprehend and consider vice with all her baits and seeming pleasures, and yet abstain, and yet distinguish, and yet prefer that which is truly better, he is the true wayfaring Christian. I cannot praise a fugitive and cloistered virtue unexercised and unbreathed, that never sallies out and seeks her adversary, but slinks out of the race, where that immortal garland is to be run for, not without dust and heat.

And I think I agree too with that passage in Bacon's essays which says:

An ant is a wise creature for itself, but it is a shrewd thing in an orchard or garden. And certainly men that are great lovers of themselves waste the public. . . . It is the wisdom of rats that will be sure to leave a house somewhat before it falls. . . . Such men are many times unfortunate. And whereas they have all their time sacrificed to themselves, they become in the end sacrifices to the inconstancy of fortune whose wings they thought by self-wisdom to have pinioned.

When I think of my own helplessness and that of most well-intentioned men, I feel like quoting that strange figure of speech from the Epistle to the Romans (vii. 24), "O wretched man that I am! Who shall deliver me from the body of this death?" And yet I have gained some assurance from the little I know in a larger way, and have seen, I think, a dim but real light. The commonly accepted attributes of God are truth, spirit (or life as distinguished from inanimate matter), immensity, infinity, and eternity; immutability, incorruptibility, omnipresence, and omnipotence; unity; and great human qualities, such as vitality, intelligence, and will. What then does it mean when one is told to love God and keep his commandments? Can you think of any better laws, principles, and commandments to keep than those derived from the attributes of God? These things are not the fabrications of theologians, but the product of the wisdom of the greatest thinkers of all the ages. For example, it is said that our duty toward men may be subsumed under the general virtues of love and righteousness, since charity toward our neighbor consists of loving him as we do ourselves and since righteousness, often misconceived of negatively, is a positive thing which demands a proper regard for the good name and the worldly welfare of our neighbor. We have thus to regulate our actions as well as our affections toward him. We shall do voluntary injury to no one. We shall avoid taking offense and, as far as practicable, shall conduct ourselves mildly and amicably toward all men. We shall be ready to forgive actual injuries when they have been identified as such and shall respect the honor of our neighbors, remembering that they too have their proper pride.

A great many things we think we owe to our neighbors, we really owe to ourselves, and I rather think that the dissemination of truth as we see it, whether as teachers or neighbors, is one of them. It would follow that those who believe us are doing us a favor and not the other way about. I think we have no right to be offended with those who reject our teachings, for what we have done we have done to satisfy our own inner urgings. We have not owed this doctrine, this enlightenment, this knowledge to anybody to be paid as a debt. We have dealt it out to satisfy ourselves. I mention this because of its possible effect on the attitudes of teachers and on their conception of the nature of their profession. It has the effect of making of teaching more of an art and less of a crusade.

Now, therefore, with the understanding that you are merely listening to me out of your own graciousness and of your own free will; also with the understanding that I claim no authority and that you do not owe me a thing on this occasion, will you let me talk to you a while about literature as a study and about some of the things I think it might do to better the conditions of society by bettering the training of youth in our institutions of higher learning? For the accomplishment of the somewhat extensive moral and personal ends I have just been discussing, literature may seem to you inadequate, and I am prepared to say that by itself I think it is. Literature is so broad and so varied that it requires as detailed and as skillful interpretation as life itself, so that almost nothing we know about nature and man will fail to have a bearing, fail to lead us to a deeper understanding of our subject. Teachers of literature, it seems to me, are the last ones who ought to tie their minds up to some narrow conception or theory, such as art for art's sake, or expressionism and impressionism, or the belief that of all poetry nothing is a poem except that which obliges the reader to construct a poem in his own imagination. Such *illuminati* remind me of animals which one sees from the train window chained to stakes in the midst of clover fields. But there is no doubt that they do a beautiful job of eating the clover which is within their range.

If then we take a becomingly modest view of the matter, what are some of the things which literary study might be expected to do in the education of the young? We have spoken of its power to appeal to the imagination.

Literature might help men and women build their worlds. Everybody who knows anything knows that we are shut away in the dark chambers of our brains and that, so far as this world is concerned, we are dependent on what our senses tell us. For determining the nature of that hypothetical external world, men resort to various practices and theories. One man resorts to his eyes and says, "Seeing is believing"; he is the scientist. Another relies on his ears and accepts what he is told; he is the traditionalist. Another relies on his senses and instincts of comfort and advantage; perhaps he is the social scientist and the man of affairs. Others resort more purely to their instincts and explain the world in terms of warfare and politics. And so on. I have explained and repeated a logical system for the determination of the truth about that world and therefore about ourselves. I think it is the best one. I explained it in terms of proof and probability and said that it concerned the judgment of all men in all their various experiences. I connected it with what is believed to be the process of thought.

We may assert with great intrepidity that it is a very important thing, what kind of world a man builds for himself or has built for him. It should, I think, be above all things a probable world. Mental health, adaptability, achievement, and happiness seem to depend upon it. When a man appears with an improbable world, say a world all bad, and denounces it, he is merely denouncing his own works and criticizing himself. Literature by the greatness of its scope, its immediacy and availability, and its interpretative nature seems to be a chief supply depot from which great probable worlds can be built. Its access is easy, and it informs men while it pleases them. There is nothing *parti pris* about great literature. It is as varied and catholic as life itself, and almost all any teacher, let us say of Shakespeare, needs to do is to ensconce himself behind his subject and let it speak.

I think also that literature has special power in teaching men to know men. If the proper study of mankind is man, and not the other way about, literature is a gift of the gods. Men are not easy to know, because they often do not wish to be known, because they do not know themselves and therefore reveal themselves wrongly, and because they cannot reveal themselves at all. But poetry, drama, and fiction lay them out for all men to view. In so far as a knowledge of the world is a knowledge of men, and it is that largely, literature is unsurpassed. It has seemed to me that literature is the only subject in the curriculum that approaches human beings as human beings directly and without intermediary.

This is an interesting matter, and I should like to pause over it for a moment. We believe that the likenesses among men are far greater than the differences, and yet we recognize that the individuality of man is his most important and most educable aspect. All men, women, and children believe themselves to be individuals and ignore, or doubt, or despise their humanity. Individuality as it normally appears is a thin thing to which they attach their greeds, their vanities, and their faults as well as their skills and virtues. It comes about that the education of the individual is largely a matter of revealing and, particularly, thickening his native-born originality. The common substance of that thickening is general humanity. This principle can be illustrated by every great human document from the Ten Commandments and the Sermon on the Mount to "The Pig Brother" and "The Little Red Hen." The ideal seems to be that a man should learn to be the master of his fate and the captain of his soul and yet say, "Da bin ich Mensch, da darf ich's sein."

The most important lessons, guideposts to happiness, tools for the tilling of the earth, and weapons in the service of the Lord are in literature for the asking. For example, literature contributes to refinement and improvement in the ways of life. By its spirit it confers liberty and by its variety it makes men fit to live in a democracy. Narrow and practical subjects do not, by virtue of their natures and aims, so readily confer these spiritual blessings. Literature may teach men to accept and make much of the need of good judgment, to make wise choices, to participate in life, and not merely to be bystanders. I think it may even enable men to face change, for it exalts courage and pictures many men in many worlds. The worshipers of the *status quo ante* are really dangerous. (See John W. Ashton, "Harsh Din and Fair Music," *Christian College Bull.*, June, 1943.) If they were content simply to shut their eyes to all that is going on—or rather like Epimetheus ever to be looking back on a world that cannot be recreated—it would be better than for them to be, as they so often are, obstructionists who do all in their power to prevent an intelligent acceptance of the significance of change. Literature may be made to teach many other things in the education of the individual, even that American youth should not expect something for nothing. As a group, it expects to gather grapes from thorns and figs from thistles. It might learn from the great tragedies of Shakespeare and the great novels of the Victorian era that it cannot do this and that it must face facts, even when these are inconvenient or unpleasant. College students ought to know that they will get out of college just what they put into it. If their minds are on athletics, dress and manners, and courting, these are the things in which they will gain proficiency. The casual things they have encountered, like the range of human learning and the fates of men, will be cast out of their minds as unrelated stuff; for the mind is an economical instrument.

Possibly the commonest expectation from humanistic study is that it will train the taste, that it will develop an art of life and an art in life. People talk about the arts of civilization, but they seldom rise to a point where they comprehend the fact that civilization is itself an art. Never in the history of the world was there so great a need for that knowledge. We speak of the American way of living, but we do not know what the features of that system are or how to apply its patterns. The humanities have an objective character. They are not only teachable, but they are excellent instruments for teaching. They are disciplinary. They relate immediately to life, and their errors yield ultimately to observation and reflection. They do this without instruments or computation, for such laboratory as they have is close at hand. True, careful, intellectual observation built the culture of the ancient world, and all that Plato and Aristotle had for the discovery of truth we still have, although we lack the will to know, the patience to observe, and the reflective reason to reconstruct. The humanities have thus at once a current of experience and a background of record.

The humanities are essentially exploratory and make a constant demand for the setting of things in order. The normal inflow to the youthful mind of today is not so much harmful or useless as jumbled. If I might borrow an expression from A. E. Housman, the minds of contemporary youth resemble nothing so much as a magpie's nest. I do not claim that the humanities have understood their own power or grasped their own function, but I do think that almost all of it might be included in the demand that they help the younger world set its mind in order. Such a setting of the mental house in order would be a necessary preliminary to effective reasoning, either creative or analytical. No field offers more constant invitation than the humanities to the association of similarities, which is the basis of genius. Indeed, artistic production in literature and the other arts goes vigorously on by its native force.

Professor Theodore M. Greene (*The Humanities After the War*, Princeton Univ. Press, 1944, pp. 36-7) declares that the humanities can and should provide a discipline in what he calls "reflective commitment." The following paragraph will serve to illustrate a whole aspect of humanistic study:

When we look at the world we live in today, we see, on the one hand, large groups of people committing themselves quickly, shortsightedly, emotionally and unreflectively, sometimes in the name of religion, sometimes in the name of patriotism, sometimes in the name of other social loyalties. And when we look at our colleges and universities, we too often find the opposite—endless reflection without sufficient recognition of the need for commitment on intellectual and spiritual questions. The humanities, if they are to accomplish what they should as human and humane activities, must educate students in the technique of reflective commitment. The successful surgeon is a fine example of such reflective commitment. When a competent surgeon is confronted with a critical case requiring immediate operation, he quickly marshals all the available medical knowledge bearing upon this particular problem. As an intelligent man, he knows perfectly well that all the evidence is not yet in, that the science of medicine knows only a fragment of all there is to know, that the best decision he can make may well be a wrong decision. But he also knows that he must make a decision, as reflectively as possible, but boldly and without hesitation. Were he to adopt the typical "academic" attitude (in the bad sense), his patient would die before he ever got around to him. What the surgeon actually does is to decide and act reflectively, resolutely, and courageously, fully aware of his own finitude and of all the risks involved.

I quote this as much for myself as for my audience, moved by the just recognition of a set of values in my subject which I myself have been disposed to minimize, complementary values as great or greater than those I have sought. I have been so greatly impressed with the importance of the consolation, rectification, and fortification afforded by literature for the problems of living that I have dwelt upon them. Indeed, in preparing this lecture I gave a somber, but I think a true, picture of the tragic possibilities of human existence. I even contended that tragedy is in the nature of things and comedy only an aspect. I said that man must act and act wisely and yet must have or achieve a certain indifference to consequences. Of course back of my opinions there lies my long study of Shakespeare. I do not believe all that Shakespeare believed, and yet I cannot get closer to the matter than by reciting what it seems to me are the tenets yielded by a fair study of his tragedies. Shakespeare inherited a crude tragedy of blood, a tragedy in which the supernatural was immanent and always ready to break through the thin wall of perception, and a tragedy whose unfailing end was death. The Elizabethans had a tradition from ancient times which put death in this position, and death was immediately present to them themselves in the facts of plague, murder, combat, and disease. Death was advertised and driven home to them by stress on funerals, wailings, ghost stories, and portents; so that they were not able to conceal, minimize, forget, or otherwise sublimate death. They had not learned any more than we have the Christian doctrine of the triumph over death, but any Elizabethan could write greatly when he wrote of death. Death was more nearly an adequate, tragic end than it is with us, for death was fate. But Shakespeare, anticipating our own times, found elements of tragedy, not in fate only, but in disaster arising from weakness and defect of character. He makes of course full use of the tragic backgrounds of life which appear in accident, untoward birth, and inescapable destiny, but he never deserts his faith in the human will and frequently lifts his defeated characters to a point where they may be said to defeat defeat.

The differences between Shakespeare's views of tragedy and ours are not very great. His views were essentially those of Aristotle, and we have little trouble accepting them. Man naturally seeks happiness, says Aristotle; but he may be mistaken in the source of happiness, which is not to be found in pleasure or riches or power, but resides in the philosophic or the good or the self-mastering mind. Man may be stricken down by fate, which may take the form of retribution, or by accident or heredity or diseas> or bereavement or the hostility of foes and tyrants. Not to find happiness as well as to meet with open disaster is tragic. All men meet a tragic end, with or without perceptible guilt. Old age is certain and, as a state, tragic. So also, loss of parents and friends, ill-health, poverty, disappointment, and hampering circumstance. But the matter is relative. A tragic event may lack importance or significance, or, having these qualities, may yet lose its power because it reveals to us something about ourselves or about human nature, human life, and human fate; or it may be merely pathetic or trivial or only remotely related to us and our lives. Man's effort to understand human life in relation to tragedy has resulted in the formation of various patterns; for example, that life is somehow good, or hopelessly bad, or a game in which the players have a fifty-fifty chance.

These inevitable issues have been very greatly and wisely exploited, not only in drama, but in poetry and fiction also, and that fact, more than almost any other, makes it important that the thoughtful reading of literature should enter into the education of the young. That is in part what is meant by the passing on from generation to generation of the tradition of our race. Now, I find that the young people of today are often very much confused and disposed to discouragement. Their wails seem to echo "Dover Beach":

. . . for the world, which seems
To lie before us like a land of dreams,
So various, so beautiful, so new
Hath really neither joy, nor love, nor light,
Nor certitude, nor peace, nor help for pain;
And we are here as on a darkling plain
Swept with confused alarms of struggle and flight,
Where ignorant armies clash by night.

Young people are unnecessarily confused. I think they need to know more than they do about the stable and relatively simple determinations of theologians, philosophers, and inspired poets as to the possibilities of existence and the rules of the game of living. No such fog hangs over us as the pessimists and the agnostics tell us. I think young people conceive of sincere living as harder than it is and that they assume responsibility for things for which they are not and can never be concerned. I have known them to respond to "Self-dependence," another poem by Matthew Arnold, and to literature which teaches humility, fortitude, and patience. It does not take much material out of which to build a castle of hope for the young, and there are no priorities. Shakespeare's spirit is so young, so indomitable, so participant that he is needed by the ages. Wordsworth has important things to say to youth, and I wish that I had time to dwell upon the greatness of his concept of man as a child of nature, moving forever onward in generations and ages of man with trees and rivers and the return of the seasons. There are the makings of a philosophy of youth in simple and ample ideas of that kind. But on this occasion I have chosen to dwell on Shakespeare and his insistence on the humanity of man.

Young people need to be taught their common humanity as well as, or even rather than, their individuality, and Shakespeare offers the great tractate in this field. The faculty of imagination is not limited by time and space or by high and low, nor is there any ultimate justification for great social barriers in a world where man's life is a span or where differences among men are so inconsiderable that, with a little remoteness, they disappear from sight like the corrugations on the skin of an orange. Although this diminishes the importance of individual peculiarities among men, it does not diminish the importance of the individual human life; but, on the contrary, by smoothing out incidental and temporal differences, it increases the importance of each human life by making it a part of humanity. *King Lear* is capable of inducing youth to forgive old age for being old, and *Romeo and Juliet* can induce old age to forgive youth for being young. "Let me not stay a jot for dinner," says Lear, "Go get it ready." Later he cries with the passionate hesitancy of old age,

> I will have such revenges on you both
> That all the world shall—I will do such things—
> What they are, yet I know not; but they shall be
> The terrors of the earth.

He utters the very appeal of age:

> I tax you not, you elements, with unkindness;
> I never gave you kingdom, call'd you children;
> You owe me no subscription. Then let fall
> Your horrible pleasure. Here I stand, your slave,
> A poor, infirm, weak, and despis'd old man;
> But yet I call you servile ministers,
> That will with two pernicious daughters join
> Your high engender'd battles 'gainst a head
> So old and white as this.

Romeo is the spirit of youth, the spirit we now rely upon to crown our arms with victory:

> Amen, amen! but come what sorrow can,
> It cannot countervail the exchange of joy
> That one short minute gives me in her sight.
> Do thou but close our hands with holy words,
> Then love devouring Death do what he dare;
> It is enough I may but call her mine.

I have been able to carry through to reasonable completeness only a few of any number of things that literary study might accomplish in education; principally that it might enable us, if not to escape the tragic fate which overhangs us in this life, at least to bear it with becoming fortitude, rather than with cowardice and a treasonable desertion of faith in the patent fact that life in this world is a natural and endurable enterprise; indeed, that life is a stage on which we may play with vigor and skill the parts which have been assigned to us. I cannot even mention the many things that it seems to me literature has done for me and for many of my pupils and fellow students in the study of this most universal of the arts.

CHAPTER VIII

THE POWER OF TRUTH

But we know in a manner nothing, by what laws storms and
tempests, earthquakes, famine, pestilence, become the instruments
of destruction to mankind. And the laws, by which persons born
into the world at such a time and place, are of such capacities,
geniuses, tempers; the laws, by which thoughts come into our mind,
in a multitude of cases; and by which innumerable things happen,
of the greatest influence upon the affairs and state of the world;
these laws are so wholly unknown to us, that we call the events which
come to pass by them, accidental; though all reasonable men know
certainly, that there cannot, in reality, be any such thing as chance.

THE METHOD of modern science has been so dominant
during the last one hundred years that we have forgotten
that there are historically any other methods of discovering
truth. It is of course obvious that the method of Galileo, Boyle,
Newton, and Watt should be used whenever it can be; but we are
forced to admit, as I showed in the first lecture of this course, that
there are regions of the human environment in which the scientific
method cannot be used for the discovery of truth. Fact-finding
studies, now so often recommended for the field of the humanities,
are at best of limited utility, for they cannot reach the core of the
humanistic subjects. Scientific method can be used in lexicography
and other philological branches, the historical method can be made
to yield results when applied to the history of literature, literary
and artistic taste can be studied by psychological and statistical
methods, and so on; but, when these methods have done the
utmost that they can do, we usually end with a body of particulars
and partial truths. The great problems of the good, the true, and
the beautiful, if I may use the ancient rubric expressive of the
ends of humanistic study, remain at best in the field of the hypothetical. The question I ask is, are we obliged to stop there? Is
there such a thing as science, organized truth, without experiment?

The world proceeded for centuries without experiment in its
quest for truth and during those centuries accomplished a great
deal in the establishment of religion, education, government, and
even in science or its equivalent. Let us take the case of the
Timaeus of Plato, which gave the world its cosmogony, and on the

whole a sound and workable cosmogony, for nearly two milleniums. Plato had a mastery of all that the world could then teach, including mathematics. He possessed a philosophic mind at once broad and acute, both creative and rational, and out of that great informed mind there came determinations of such probability that they bid fair to outlast the ages. They still have truth in them and possess both applicability and consistency. It was Plato who announced the principle that nations should be governed by laws and not by men, that morals are one and the same in essence, so that nations and individuals have essentially one code. It was he who discovered the principle of perfection in the midst of the trial and error which characterize the aims and actions of men. Amongst other things he determined on general grounds of enlightened reason and expressed in the *Timaeus* a probable organization of the universe. The particular shortcomings of Plato's cosmogony are as nothing compared to its essential rightness.

So it is that, in our efforts to know the truth in the fields difficult of scientific exploitation, we are not helpless or without illustrious guides in the history of civilization and the advancement of science. I have suggested that our reliance be on superior thought, and it may be worth while at this time to make a simple statement of the general principles of the psychology of genius. We shall not of course attempt anything either definite or technical in such a field. We shall resort again, because of its simplicity, to the principles laid down by William James and admit that we personally are not competent to go further except by the citation of other authorities, a thing which on this occasion is not necessary.

In order not to drag out a familiar thing unduly, let us quote a few sentences from James's *Principles of Psychology* (II, 360-61):

Genius, then, as has been already said, *is identical with the possession of similar association to an extreme degree.* Professor Bain says: "This I count the leading fact of genius. I consider it quite impossible to afford any explanation of intellectual originality except on the supposition of unusual energy on this point." Alike in the arts, in literature, in practical affairs, and in science, association by similarity is the prime condition of success.

But as, according to our view, there are two stages in reasoned thought, one where similarity merely *operates* to call up cognate thoughts, and another farther stage, where the bond of identity between the cognate thoughts is *noticed*; so *minds of genius may be divided into two main sorts, those who notice the bond and those who merely obey it.* The first are the abstract reasoners, properly so called, the men of science, and philosophers—the analysts, in a word; the latter are the poets, the critics—the artists, in a word, the men of intuitions. These judge rightly, classify cases, characterize them by the most striking analogic epithets, but go no further.   At first sight it might seem that the analytic mind represented simply a higher intellectual stage, and that the intuitive mind represented an arrested stage of intellectual development; but the difference is not so simple as this.   Professor Bain has said that a man's advance to the scientific stage (the stage of noticing and abstracting the bond of similarity) may often be due to an *absence* of certain emotional sensibilities.

James then goes on to discuss intellectual power and leaves his readers with the impression, as other authorities do, that insight may reveal hidden truth.

We shall pass over also the world-old resort to revelation and shall think of it as an aspect of authority, although it connects itself closely with the doctrine of intuition.   We know that the world from the time of Plato, and especially his pupil Aristotle, subsisted on authority, developing older teachings and of course in many cases adding to them, adding error as well as truth.   We know that a vast system of science, known now as scholasticism or Aristotelianism, arose on the foundation of authority and existed until the time of Francis Bacon.   Indeed, we know that it did not go to pieces at once from his attack, but receded and grew discredited before the onslaught of his followers, who were experimental scientists, and was ultimately rejected.   We know also, in spite of the errors committed in his name, that Aristotle was a great thinker, scientist, and discoverer.   We would do well also to remember that Aristotle was, so far as we know, practically without instruments and produced his great works by means of his unaided senses and reasoning faculties.   All that Aristotle had as a searcher for truth every man is born with.   I say this in order that we who desire to know and understand, even quite difficult things, may not despair.

The question I now ask is, not whether scholasticism or Aristotelianism still has an applicability in the determination of truth, but whether science, which is progress in organized knowledge, is possible without experiment; that is, whether the natural synthetical determinations of enlightened reason may not still have validity, may not be worthy of profound respect, and may not still offer us a ground and basis for procedure and a way out in our humanistic studies in the modern world.

It is obvious that in this matter Descartes should come up for consideration, and, although I am not ready to announce a neo-cartesianism, I do think that some illumination may come from the author of *De Methodo*. We know that for a considerable time Descartes was the champion of the dying Aristotelianism. We know also that his method was mathematical and that Cartesian physics is obviously less probable than Newtonian physics. The question is rather whether Cartesian as well as Platonic principles may not still have a value in coming to understand the world. Descartes declared that matter and ideas were the same, that an atom as an indivisible particle was an impossibility. He developed a theory of vortices to explain all physical phenomena, and announced the principles of the conservation of movement. He seems to have anticipated our latest physics, but these matters do not concern us here. (See Rufus Suter, "Science Without Experiment: A Study of Descartes," *The Scientific Monthly*, April, 1944, pp. 265-68.)

The Cartesian method rests on intuition. It demands "clear and distinct ideas," and in the first principle of Descartes' method he declares that he would not "accept anything for true which I did not know to be such." His remaining principles, though clearly mathematical in nature, are not perhaps to be thrown into the discard by thinkers in other fields. He would "divide each of the difficulties under examination into as many parts as possible and as might be necessary for its adequate solution." He would commence "with objects the simplest and easiest to know" and ascend step by step to a knowledge of the complex. In every case he would "make enumerations so complete and reviews so general, that I might be assured that nothing was omitted." This may be outworn Cartesianism, but I respectfully commend it to those who aspire to either scholarship or scientific research.

It may seem to you that I have waded in beyond my depth, but in point of fact I have not gone far enough to be in the least danger. I wish I were able to render my somewhat vague ideas much more definite than I can. I have the idea that we American academicians are not living up to our full possibilities either in teaching or research. I have suggested that we ought to know more about the universe and the world in which we live, that we ought to set our minds free by the exercise of imagination, that we ought to aspire to higher things, and that we ought to operate with increased intensity. I think that we can accomplish a great deal. When I think of the history of our profession and of our present facilities and advantages, I am far from hopeless. There is at present a great deal at stake, and I cannot help thinking of

our situation in terms of crisis. I think of an approach in terms
only of the simplest human virtues—industry, sincerity, and
intelligence. I think we need the will to achieve:

And the will therein lieth, which dieth not. Who knoweth the mysteries
of the will, with its vigor? For God is but a great will pervading all things
by nature of its intentness. Man doth not yield himself to the angels, nor
unto death utterly, save only through the weakness of his feeble will.

This famous quotation from "Joseph Glanvill" which Poe
prefixes to his story *Ligeia* reminds me that I am able to draw
from the field of my own scholarly work a suggestive illustration
of the possibilities of the superior intellectual power which I have
tried to describe and which I wish to invoke. You will understand of course that I am not recommending merely a quest for
the highest genius in our universities, but that I believe that
superior intellect is needed at every level of human culture and
in every station of human life. If we can by united effort raise
the intellectual level of American universities, which is a thing
that could be done, we may let the highest genius take care of itself.

Edgar Allan Poe has long been under-rated as an intellectual
force. He has been described as shallow and pretentious only, but
the results of more impartial recent investigation have been to
make us aware that he was a man, not only of the most perspicaci-
ous intellect, but of very extensive knowledge. He had worked
out a principle of unity which he carried into the realm of organized
structure. He believed that the power of analysis in no sense
destroys the essential meaning of imagination but rather contributes to it. He had an early and continued liking for natural
science, and aspired to interpret intuitively a mass of scientific
detail according to what he believed to be the law which governs
the universe. He felt that we, as existing in time, stand in the
middle part of the creative process in a period in which constituent
atoms or elements exhibit themselves in a state of great complexity.

The consequence was that in *Eureka* he made a bold and by
no means futile attempt to solve the problem of the universe. It
is pretty generally admitted that Poe anticipated some of the discoveries of the new physics. His facilities for solving this greatest
of scientific problems were not, humanly speaking, very great,
but his courageous effort is nevertheless worthy of every respectful
attention. He had gone over with his quick and masterly intelligence a considerable body of scientific writings, including all
current theories of cosmology—Newton, Laplace, Ferguson, von

Humboldt, Dick, Coleridge, and encyclopedic works, old and new. To say that he had done no work as a scientist with his own hands or that his training was deficient, is to discredit his intellect. He had understood with clarity and had thought with perspicacity. Such a man as Poe, we may believe, needs less systematic training in order to achieve comprehension than do men of inferior genius. Thus toward the end of his life he made this actual attempt to state what he had learned and what he had thought out on the basis of his study. It is a characteristic attempt, valiant, perhaps overbold, in which he begins by renouncing both induction and deduction and declaring in favor of a procedure based on intuition and pure theory. This procedure he sought to elevate into position, not as a scientific method, but as the one scientific method by which the human mind may arrive at truth.

Now, an interesting thing about the enterprise is that Poe knew what he was really doing. He reveals in his rather touching little preface that he knew that he had been working as a poet:

> To the few who love me and I love—to those who feel rather than to those who think—to dreamers and those who put faith in dreams as the only realities—I offer this Book of Truths, not in its character of Truth-Teller, but for the Beauty that abounds in its Truth; constituting it true. To these I present the composition as an Art-Product alone:—let us say as a Romance; or, if I be not urging too lofty a claim, as a Poem.

Whatever you may have been taught to think of Poe, let me point out to you that there is nowhere to be found since Francis Bacon greater intellectual courage and greater faith in the possibilities of the human mind. I wish that we had more of Poe's faith and more of his industry, not that we might each of us attempt to solve the problems of the cosmos, but that we might attempt to solve the major problems of existence which confront us, our pupils, and our generation. There are many problems before us about which I should like to know the truth, for I believe the truth will set us free. I believe that back of darkness and confusion there shines a light of truth. I believe that it is possible for every man to behold that light and by its beam to realize the aim and purpose of his existence. If any man says, "There is no need of such a light," I can only say, "You do not speak the truth," or say, "Your eyes are blind." Many men rely vaguely on the advancement of science, and up to a certain point the faith is good, but there are problems which science cannot solve, and even science can do nothing for drifters and doubters and for those who follow quacks and charlatans or who are ill with the greater maladies.

For example, I should like to ask again an ancient question, and I shall put it in terms of the Shorter Catechism and ask, What is the chief end of man? I prefer to reply to that question in terms of the document itself rather than to offer any of the many other current replies expressed or implied. The Catechism says that the chief end of man is to glorify God and keep his commandments. I shall reserve the right to interpret this answer for myself on rather liberal theological lines, but I think that as an answer it is much better than its rivals. Our country has grown frivolous as it has grown rich and has substituted the moving picture palace for the church. It has exalted the ancient vice of cupidity and made Mammon its god. It has placed before the young an ideal of wilfulness and pleasure-seeking instead of obedience to law. We have not been able to stand prosperity, and we have been headed downhill. It will do no good for me to denounce these evils, for I shall not be believed, or those who do believe will be as powerless as I. I have thought about this matter and have brought to you in this course of lectures the idea that our situation may be saved, if it needs salvation, or bettered, if it needs only betterment, by a renewed and determined development and application of intellect to our situation, both individual and general.

I presume that, if we recommend such an effort to understand in order to improve, it is appropriate to inquire whether or not it is a feasible cause, a practicable operation. St. Paul in his writings puts great stress on faith, and only the very narrow would limit what he says to a strictly religious application. A thing which has impressed me as a teacher is the necessity of faith if we are to live happily and successfully in the world. The inertia of the young, and many of our young people are inert, seems to me to come about in part because they are perplexed or because they actually distrust. They do not believe that this is a probable or even a possible world, nor that the sum of human life is somehow good. They have been told that this is an utterly new age, that everything is different now, and that everything is in confusion. It seems to me that the chief moral task of the teacher in this age is to convince his pupils that this is a world in which something can be done. I became finally convinced of this while I was in the military forces of the United States.

Young people are told both by actions and words that religion is a back number and that the church no longer exercises the power it used to exercise in the world. They are not told that Christianity has always been under fire and that its high and uncompromising idealism has always provoked opposition. They are told that the standard curriculum of the sciences and the liberal arts is outmoded and that it is desirable to study in college only those things which will serve them in practical life. They have not been told of the long struggle of culture against barbarism and have not heard Bacon say that studies "teach not their own use; but that is a wisdom without them and above them, won by observation"; or, in other words, that studies cease to be studies as soon as they become strictly utilitarian. They are not told that this age is not new in any essential particular, that it merely has some new gadgets and a few new ways of committing old sins. The age is not new. The regions of personal conduct and character and the regions of the family, the neighborhood, and the state are almost unaltered. The problems in these areas have undergone little change in the later centuries, and they do not promise to be much affected by modern inventions. They are the regions in which man spends most of his time. Shakespeare taught me how unchanging the essentials of human life and human nature are.

Most of our failure in what I have called faith has come and will continue to come from ignorance. There are many forms of ignorance, and the least objectionable is pure ignorance. Those who are lowly and have always been unprivileged are apt to develop a wisdom of their own. The ignorant who think they know and do not are the scourge and despair of all good men. Our country is, I think, particularly full of extremely ignorant persons who think they know everything. As time has gone on, so many of the older ideas have been discarded, like useless furniture, that we now get along with a very small number of ideas, not all bad, but all tenaciously held and serving to block the entry of all liberal thought. It is doubtful if the entire stock of ideas held by our statesmen, educators, and editors during an entire year would serve the purposes of a really great thinker for a single day. Everywhere there are the massed forces of hostile and indifferent ignorance.

Another ancient enemy of enlightenment is corruption, based on self-indulgence and selfishness. We need not dwell upon it, for our age is no worse in these respects than other ages have been;

possibly it is a great deal better. Americans are usually self-respecting and polite, and I believe, from a fairly wide acquaintance with my country, that American life is essentially sound. We have never lived like Germans or Roumanians, or other degenerate modern nations; but we need not thank God we are not as other men, for we have always the lively fear that we have been rapidly getting worse.

Another class of people who offer opposition to faith in life may be described as men who are the victims of self-conceit. They are sometimes doctors, scientists, and men who operate in the realm of mechanical manipulation. They have learned to operate in a section of the material universe, and they conclude that they are superior to their fellow men in other lines of activity and thought. Some of the worst of these intellectual curmudgeons are to be found in university faculties. Such men are described as being "fed up," and they are impermeable. They would never listen to a mere professor of English literature or imagine that a man in such a field could have anything to say worthy of their attention. They are not scholars and scientists; real scholars and scientists are not like that, but are men at once of humility and intellectual curiosity. These narrow-minded men usually exploit their subjects only as these subjects conduce to their own advantage and profit. They get a sort of god-complex. It has come about in the modern world that man is God's chief rival. They take too narrow a view of God and all the universe. The thing is not so small, so simple, and so one-sided as they make it.

> If the red slayer think he slays,
>   Or if the slain think he is slain,
> They know not well the subtle ways
>   I keep and pass and turn again.
>
> Far or forgot to me is near;
>   Shadow and sunlight are the same;
> The vanished gods to me appear;
>   And one to me are shame and fame.
>
> They reckon ill who leave me out:
>   When me they fly, I am the wings;
> I am the doubter and the doubt,
>   And I the hymn the Brahmin sings.
>
> The strong gods pine for my abode,
>   And pine in vain the sacred Seven;
> But thou, meek lover of the good,
>   Find me, and turn thy back on heaven.

There is a good deal about the modern world in which our students live which, without interpretation, might serve to convince them that there is such a thing as fundamental social injustice. I do not think that, when all powers have been permitted to play and all the scores are in, there is such a thing. I think that we get, even in this world, in the long run just about what we are entitled to get. I need to bolster my faith by use of various principles, such as William James's statement that the most intelligent creature is the one which is actuated by the most distant ends, but I do believe that whatsoever a man soweth that shall he also reap. Students do see daily the prizes of student life go to wealth, fashion, athletic prowess rather than to diligence in study. But students do not know the whole story. They do not know that a court of experience will one day sit to determine these cases and that its judgment is bound to be just. Study is long and hard. It demands self-denial and real labor. It makes a man frowsy and abstracted, often slow in the up-take of student conviviality; but in the end it pays a student to be diligent in his business. I should like our earnest-minded students, who are the only ones that really count, to have faith that things will usually come out right in the end. It is impossible to see the whole picture, and no one should try to hasten the sometimes slow processes of ultimate justice. There are many concealed factors and a scheme of rightness in things, which only the mystics seem able to see. Blake, for example, gives expression to this strange unity and interdependence, not in matter only, but in immaterial things. Observe it in these lines from "Auguries of Innocence":

> To see the world in a grain of sand,
> And a heaven in a wild flower;
> Hold infinity in the palm of your hand,
> And eternity in an hour.

> A robin redbreast in a cage
> Puts all heaven in a rage;
> A dove-house filled with doves and pigeons
> Shudders hell through all its regions.
> A dog starved at his master's gate
> Predicts the ruin of the state. . .
> A horse misused upon the road
> Calls to heaven for human blood.
> Every wolf's and lion's howl
> Raises from hell a human soul.
> Each outcry of the hunted hare
> A fibre from the brain doth tear.

A skylark wounded on the wing,
A cherubim does cease to sing. . . .
The wild deer wandering here and there,
Keeps the human soul from care.

A few bold and cynical minds may contend that all is irrational, that all happens by chance, or, if there is any plan, it does not reveal itself as logical to man. Others a bit more imaginatively creative will personify the forces at work in the world as orderly fate or whimsical fortune. The scientific and thinking mind is likely, even with little knowledge, to keep faith in a hidden order of the universe, hoping that we may one day understand the plan. The religious mind is inclined to appreciate its own inadequacies and limited understandings and to place the universe in control of a rational deity. Mistress Quickly says, "God's a good man," and I am sure he is no less than a good man. I am sure that the knowledge of what we may call the laws of God is the essence of truth and that human happiness lies in the knowledge of those laws and in conformity to them. I have said that originality is the discovery of truth, and, if it is, it is also the discovery of happiness or freedom or salvation or whatever the heart may desire. It therefore comes about that Milton's great proposal is not his end and purpose only, but the end and purpose of human thought. He prayed,

That, to the highth of this great argument,
I may assert Eternal Providence,
And justify the ways of God to men.

I should like to state a few simple reasons why we might be justified in entering upon even so stern a quest of truth as I have recommended. The first is that we might convince ourselves that this is God's world. In this search I would not have you neglect the religious and theological systems which have gathered unto themselves the wisdom of innumerable thinkers. Men have been engaged on this matter of the existence and nature of God since they appeared upon earth. No question has been more earnestly and honestly thought about. No subject has less superstition in it than has theology. I had early religious instruction which I think was very sound and very valuable to me. I was taught to face facts and to expect the worst of myself, in which particular the teaching was not wrong. I was taught to see the inexorability of natural law and the certainty of judgment in accordance with moral law. I can easily believe in the survival of the fittest, and I endorse the justice of the dictum. I am no theologian of course, but my early experience made me think intelligently of God, because I seemed to see manifestations of his activity in the world in which I lived. I never thought of him sentimentally or anthropomorphically.

Secondly, there is, I believe, a road to faith in the ultimate truth of things, what we might call the honesty of the universe, in the study of nature. Nature, as I understand it, is uniform. Its forces always work according to their several laws. There is a spirit of growth and power throughout the universe which is thought of as the chief activity of God. Wherever nature is ascertained and tested it is found to be faithful. Why, therefore, if we observe natural laws and get results with certainty, should we not, if we observe moral laws, believe also that results will follow with equal certainty? Our limits will arise from the nature of the moral laws we obey. Proof of their validity may not be forthcoming, but in the highest wisdom we find abundant probability. I think we are entitled to every faith that good lives mean happiness and bad lives mean misery. But this can be true only as a matter of averages. I am aware that the problem as I have stated it here is over-simplified. We pay for other people's sins as well as our own and are held responsible for our evil deeds even though we committed them in ignorance or with good intentions. Life is a vaster, a more perilous, and a more dubious thing than any man can comprehend. The dangers and penalties of existence remain, and the tragedy of innocent young men as logs for the burning even now stares us in the face.

Thirdly, there is that strange emotional state called loyalty, which when supported by reason becomes itself a substantial human motive and a ground of faith. We wish to fight on the right side. We prefer to be on the side of God and his saints rather than on the side of persecutors, exploiters, and materialists. In my case you need not regard this as merely ideal aspiration, for I have worn the uniform of my country's army. I believe there is much value in the idea of God as a center of loyalty as well as of truth. I believe it is a road to faith in living. It is not for nothing that we long to come to the aid of the Lord against the mighty.

I have now brought you into a region where you will see that we need a kind of knowledge which cannot be supplied by the laboratory. I do not for that reason despise the laboratory, but

I do perceive the need for a high supplementary intelligence. The gist of what I have been trying to say this afternoon and in this course of lectures is that enlightenment, as wide and free and perfect as possible, is the chief hope of the world. Perhaps there is a *non sequitur* in my thinking, but I can suggest nothing else, and I certainly have a powerful authoritative backing.

This enlightenment brings into being the thought that, since there is unquestionably a great power operating in the world, this power may reach down into the most intimate life of the individual, and the heart of man may be illuminated by the truth of God. We are a part of nature, and we do not know the whole story. We do not know all the ramifications and connections. But we may sagely believe that the destiny of the universe is our destiny and that the laws of the universe govern us; so that a wise, competent, and intelligent man may believe that his affairs and his fate are not merely accidental. This is but an aspect of relativism, and, strangely enough, one that is borne out by the testimony of the saints.

Secondly, it follows that straight thinking, which means thinking which is in conformity to truth, is the only possible basis for human conduct. Error and sin are largely the same. Aristotle knew this. All the great moral philosophers have known it. It was in Milton's imagination when he depicted the sin of Eve as due, not so much to willful disobedience and sensual appetite, as to fallacious thinking. It is doubtful if any man can commit evil without first deceiving himself.

In the third place, there is nothing bound, patterned, and repetitious about the individual human intellect. A man's mind may be in chains, it often is; but when it is free, honest, and bold, it moves over the universe like the spirit of God over the primordial waters. I have tried to tell you in these lectures that it is a greater instrument than any or many of us think it is. I have thought that we whose business it is to educate others, should have a noble and ample conception of the possibilities of the mind. I have suggested that we teachers of literature should put our hearts and our wills behind this higher faith in the possibilities of human endeavor and achievement.

The things I have urged are not, however, merely matters of polite persuasion toward general culture and right living. They have also profound importance in the future of the American republic. The bases of democracy are primarily two: first, the rights of man, which is an idea from the region of moral philosophy; and, secondly, the dignity of man, which is a religious idea. The hypothesis of the rights of man is not capable of scientific demonstration and yet is an absolute essential to the perpetuation of our democratic government. Our culture must be deep enough and broad enough for our people as a whole to understand and therefore keep alive the idea. We must train citizens who believe in the moral law and know why they believe in it. The only liberty which it is safe for any civilized people to exercise is liberty under the law. There are no natural rights if there is no moral law. American liberty in its essence is not sentiment or unrestrained individualism; it is a regulated liberty which has for its aim the protection and the welfare of the whole people. These aims cannot be accomplished with anything less than an educated and moral population. We must believe in the validity of what we teach, and in order to believe we must also know.

The other law of democracy, the dignity of man, was bred and fostered through generations of Christian living and Christian thinking. A vicious, ignorant race cannot maintain it. We must remember as a great law of nature that no mind is free to reject the truth and that truth needs continually to be ascertained and presented. Truth thus becomes our chief instrument in the perpetuation of democracy, which we believe to be the most natural and the justest way for men to live together in society. If anything at all may be true, if we distrust all human knowledge, if we have no knowledge and no faith, we teachers can teach nothing, and our American republic will suffer. The moral and political bases of democracy are known and comprehensible. They are sustained by generations of experience and are in conformity with the nature of man. It would be a sad spectacle to see our democratic principles saved on the field of battle only to decay among our people in times of peace. There are other ideas for the government of men, but there is none so much in line with human nature, at least with the nature of western peoples, as is democracy. What our republic needs more than anything else is a knowledge of its own principles and a faith in their validity. To say that these things will take care of themselves is a very questionable statement.

In order to bring these ideas closer to the question at issue, let me quote a paragraph from *Freedom and the Liberal Arts* by Wendell L. Willkie (New York, 1943). He is speaking of the influence of the German university on American higher education.

And it has been a harmful influence. It has encouraged the sacrifice of methods that make for wide intelligence to those which are concerned only with highly specialized knowledge; it has held that the subject is more important than the student; that knowledge is more important than understanding; that science, in itself, can satisfy the soul of man; and that intelligent men should not be allowed to concern themselves with politics and the administration of state. Such matters should be left to trained politicians.

He then quotes from President Hopkins of Dartmouth the statement that "it would be a tragic paradox if, as a result of the war, we were to allow our system of higher education to be transformed into the type of education which has made it so easy for a crowd of governmental gangsters like Hitler's outfit to commandeer a whole population."

In this course of lectures I have conceived of literature as a broad record of human action, observation, thought, and feeling—almost as broad as life itself. Because it is so varied, I have recognized that it makes extensive demands on those who presume to interpret it. I have said specifically that I think teachers of literature in institutions of higher learning need to know a great deal about the whole modern *studium generale*, the whole range of human learning, and to understand, at least fundamentally, nature and life as they have been studied in their various aspects. I even said that, with the advancement of learning, there has been a great simplification of concepts and inter-relations, so that the job of acquiring an excellent general education is an easier and a more comprehensible job than it used to be. My position is, that in order to interpret literature, which is an infinitely varied record of nature and human life, a man should know as well as he can what nature and human life are actually like. I was therefore disposed to deprecate too great specialization within the field of literature or within that of general human learning, particularly early specialization, and I called attention to the fact that men and women do not achieve maturity and become ready for intelligent specialization until they are twenty-one or twenty-two years old. My inference as to the ordinary college course was patent.

Without discrediting in any way other approaches to literature, such as the philological, the historical, or the aesthetic, I recommended, as most in conformity with the experience and the environment of man, the approach to literature by way of the discovery of truth in terms of probability and proof. You may remember that I quoted Bishop Butler to the effect that "probability is the very guide of life." I thought of philology, the history of literature, and aesthetic criticism as being, all of them with other methods, capable of being subsumed under the quest for truth. I had already made it clear that the humanities are as yet, and perhaps forever will be, limited in their search for truth to the determination of the probable.

Because the field to be covered is so extensive, because we cannot hope to succeed in our educational task without industry and the entertainment of high ideals, and because I saw many destructive and obstructive elements, both old and new, blocking our way, I entered strongly into the moral field. I discussed in moral terms our institutions and our academic life. I make no apology for doing this, because it is an obvious thing to do. We really need greater industry, greater seriousness, and higher aims.

Finally, I have carried through these lectures a theory of the mental life which is both sound and practicable. According to it, if we rely upon superior intelligence, our reliance will not be in vain. If we lay a broader and stronger foundation for humanistic studies, if we operate boldly and imaginatively, we may hope that greater minds will, as time goes on, yield greater syntheses and that all minds will gain, along with increased understanding, increased power in adapting themselves to environment and making greater use of it in the promotion of human happiness. "Duty and interest are perfectly coincident; for the most part in this world, but entirely and in every instance if we take in the future, and the whole; this being implied in the notion of a good and perfect administration of things."

CHAPTER IX

THE EQUIPMENT OF THE SCHOLAR*

Then after we have judged the very best we can, the evidence upon which we must act, if we live and act at all, is perpetually doubtful to a very high degree. And the constitution and course of the world in fact is such, as that want of impartial consideration what we have to do, and venturing upon extravagant courses, because it is doubtful what will be the consequence, are often naturally, i.e. providentially, altogether as fatal, as misconduct occasioned by heedless inattention to what we certainly know, or disregarding it from overbearing passion.

I SHOULD LIKE to begin this lecture by discussing with you some crucial aspects of graduate study as now carried on in American universities, its principles and practices, and at a later time in the lecture I shall take up specifically the subject of the equipment of the scholar.

I ought to preface what I am going to say by admitting that I do not know very much about graduate study at this university or anywhere in other departments than my own. What I have to say, however, is, I believe, sound in principle and may therefore find some application in other departments than English, particularly in those whose fields are also discursive. I fear that we are deficient in both aim and method, and I am not so diffident that I am not willing to say that our shortcomings are widely characteristic of graduate work throughout the country. I should like to begin by endeavoring to clarify the aim of graduate study without, however, entering very fully into the details of the subject.

As I look over the field of graduate study, I see only one factor that serves to discriminate graduate study from undergraduate study, although there are certain elements in our situation that seem to render it impractical for us to limit ourselves exclusively to that one characteristic element. The factor I refer to is research; that is, careful or critical inquiry or examination in seeking facts or principles.

Attempts have been and are being made in a few American universities to substitute formal criticism or literary composition

*Lecture before the Graduate English Club of the University of Washington.

for research as a basis of graduate study and as an occasion for the granting of graduate degrees, that is, to substitute an activity whose basis is manner and the exploitation of individual feeling and opinion for an activity directed toward the discovery of truth. There may be, I am sure, good reason for the pursuit of these aims, but what I call attention to is that they are different from research in their nature and educational utility. They are not directed toward the discovery of new knowledge, the acquisition of the habit of loving and seeking truth for its own sake, and the perpetuation and re-establishment of the learned tradition of the race. Scholars operate traditionally as men of learning and back of us lie centuries of characteristic activity. We are professionally not called upon to become poets and creative artists. We have our traditional service as teachers as well as scholars to render, and, however lowly our profession may be in the eyes of persons of different and possibly higher talents, I for one am disposed to accept membership in a profession which is ancient, necessary, and often noble.

It will at least be admitted that these forms of intellectual activity, authorship and literary criticism, are different from research and that we as graduate teachers are widely committed to research as our object; also that the larger number of us neither will nor can substitute anything else for research as the end and aim of our professional lives; nor are willing to grant that, let us say, the composition of an epic poem or the writing of a work of fiction, however admirable and praiseworthy these things may be, are properly recognized by awarding of the Ph.D. degree. It is not so much that we have great admiration for the Ph.D. as that we think that the highest degree in course should be reserved for the particular thing for which it has come to stand in the educated world. It is certainly less confusing to preserve the distinction than to obliterate it.

Now, these extremes can be made to serve on this occasion to make clear the qualities of true and false graduate study as ordinarily practiced. If we as scholars do our work badly, we are as guilty as those who would put research out of the picture and are actually less frank and manly than are the avowed enemies of research. It therefore behooves us to keep constantly in mind the quality as well as the methods of research.

How do these two things, artistic creation and methodical discovery of truth, differ from each other? If we can get some light on that question, we may at least enjoy the scholar's satisfaction of knowing where we are and whither we are tending, so that in the words of Webster we can better tell what to do and how to do it. Certainly it is no question of better or worse, but is rather a matter of two separate and justifiable modes of professional behavior, sometimes even happily united in the same individual. The question is simple enough, and the answer has been known for generations. I shall give you a brief explanation of it derived from James (*Principles of Psychology*, II, 360-71), who in turn followed Bain. There are, he says, two stages of reasoned thought, one where similar association merely operates to call up cognate thoughts, and the other where the reason notices the bond of identity between the thoughts evoked. Those whose emotional sensibilities arrest the process and whose aesthetic nature demands expression of the concrete images, are the artists. Those who go further by nature or choice in the true process of reasoning are the analysts, the scholars and scientists. Often enough, as I said, the two abilities are united in one man. Some artists do have the power to think through their representations, or if you prefer to put it so, have the ability voluntarily to arrest their analytical powers at a creative level or the ability to shove them forward, if they choose, into the field of analysis. I presume, however, that men are usually of one type or the other, and it becomes the chief pleasure of the student of the history of literature to spend his time explaining to the world and even to himself what his less rational brother has really said or tried to say in terms of concrete images.

In the program of courses accepted for graduate credit in graduate schools there are actually many courses in which there is and can be no element of research. For example, in my training I received graduate credit for elementary Sanskrit, elementary Old Norse, Gothic, and Old French as well as for many advanced, general informational courses. From such courses arises the popular idea that a graduate course is merely a harder course than an undergraduate course. But these propaedeutic and informational courses are not distinguishable intellectually in any way from undergraduate courses. If one accepts the only discoverable criterion of graduate study, one is bound to accept the dictum, "no research, no graduate study." It follows that research courses should be carefully and consciously distinguished from others both by administrative authorities and by those who conduct such courses. It may also follow that genuine graduate courses are far fewer than we think or admit, and it certainly follows that such courses should enter strongly and definitely into every graduate program. Unless we recognize them when we see them, we can hardly administer a genuine graduate school.

I enter now into a more particular field which I shall designate as method.

One may say quite generally that the attitude, the conditions, and the eventuation of this body of instruction should be adjusted to research and the teaching of the methods of research.

Stated simply, one might say that one primary difference between graduate and undergraduate courses is that in the former the students, and not the professor, must do the work. In undergraduate teaching this is only relatively true. Lecturing and good teaching in general are economical of time in the imparting of information, the awakening of interest, the arousing of imagination, and the cultivation of judgment. In research, however, the attitude is entirely different. No graduate teacher engaged in a research course ought to lecture to graduate students except for the purposes of making clear the line between the known and the unknown (in other words, the delineation and determination of problems) and for giving instruction in methods of research; possibly also, as Dr. Woodrow Wilson used to say, for making trial trips, or illustrations of research in practice. Even method, since every problem requires its own method of solution, may usually be attended to better by private conference than by lectures on method. Nevertheless I am willing to admit that graduate teachers may find it convenient and profitable to give lectures on method. The essence of the matter, however, is the location and delineation of problems and the attack upon these problems by the students themselves.

Secondly, conditions should be favorable. There should be time and at least the semblance of leisure for the opening of questions, the consideration of methods of attack, and an atmosphere of sufficient informality to promote thought and provoke originality. If I bring a Shakespeare play before my seminar, spend as much time as may be necessary to state the unsolved problems connected with that play, and assign these problems to various members of my seminar for attempted solution, I may sit back with a clear conscience and listen for days to their reports and at the end come out and see them come out with closer approximations to the truth than we had at the beginning. In practice it often happens that discoveries are made, for we have deliberately put ourselves in the way of making discoveries.

Another condition working strongly against sound and productive graduate study in many places is the ideal of covering in course work the whole field, a worthy ideal in itself and one professionally useful if the candidates for degrees subsequently become teachers. But in the meantime it militates against research by creating a vast routine for the acquisition of knowledge and the checking of this knowledge by numerous examinations, examinations which bring with them their psychology of formalism and fear. I think it would be much better for research and productivity and in the end achieve the object more certainly if, instead of putting on graduate students so heavy a burden of required courses, we sought to make our students masters of the methods of research, permeated with the love of truth, habituated to study, and filled with the aspiration to excellence. The matter is under present conditions a relative one, but the fact remains that such graduates can work up neglected fields as they need them. A good Ph.D. ought to be able and willing to write a doctor's dissertation every year during the rest of his life—a somewhat horrible thought. I therefore recommend that we endeavor to cut down the enormous course requirement for doctoral candidates which now prevails and do away with present meticulous divisions of our subject into so many separate fields. These specializations within a field like English or history are really quite absurd, since there is no reason why any man cannot master the whole of these subjects or any part of them if he is a properly qualified worker. Let us put our attention on research rather than the acquisition of knowledge; and let us quit this absurd business of limiting the resort of graduate students to single individuals within a department on the ground that these men are the only men competent to direct research in a particular segment of a particular field. The present situation merely breeds intradepartmental jealousies unbecoming in scholars and often subjects candidates for degrees to unfair attacks directed, not against them themselves, but against the men who have assumed responsibility for their theses. If I were the dean of a graduate school, I should see to it that every man who comes up shall have been in contact with every scholar in his field, whether in his department or not, who is in any way qualified to assist that candidate in the preparation of his thesis.

Finally, I wish to speak of the desirability, indeed the necessity, of opening means for publication to our graduate students. I shall say little about it, but on both sides it is mandatory. The candidate needs the experience, the inspiration, and the material advantage which arise from publication. Publication is a special operation and very instructive. On the other hand, the university needs to have credit for what it does and to have its record written down where men may read it. Scholars need to read it. It is good for the state of learning that they should do so; and the university which fails to make known its activities loses reputation, opportunity, and the inspiration to achieve. Let us quit filing doctor's dissertations away in the library. Let us publish always, and as a regular part of the exercise, at least those parts of every dissertation which contribute to the sum of human knowledge or determine with certainty principles which have hitherto been vague and uncertain or unknown.

The equipment of the scholar depends in varying degrees on the field which the scholar intends to exploit; but, since I conceive of the field of modern literature as one, I am disposed to set forth a fairly extensive ideal in the matter of the scholar's achievement. I am persuaded that the curse of higher education in our time is low ideals, and the specific purpose before me during these current weeks is to urge upon my colleagues and pupils higher aspirations, greater care in planning, and greater confidence in the possibility of achievement. The time for gaining preparation is in most cases limited and the burden is considerable, for schooling has often been deficient. I have therefore thought that a good deal of the necessary equipment is best gained in the midst of scholarly work. Indeed, I see some advantages in this procedure, which is a natural and practical way of gaining it. A foreign language, for example, which a graduate student has to use in work on his problem becomes a mere tool and not an end in itself, and it has always seemed to me that foreign languages are best learned when regarded in that way. The scholar, faced with a language barrier to his progress, simply sets aside a period of eight or ten weeks, which he devotes intensively to the language and comes out with an adequate mastery. I know that it might be better if all students had the benefits of training in the best elementary and preparatory schools, but the fact remains that they usually have not. They owe it to themselves to make the best of a situation which is rendered worse by exaggerating the difficulty. They have decided to devote themselves to scholarship, and the obstacles are usually not insurmountable.

The profession of scholarship is a continuous one from age to age, although we do have certain periods when scholarship has been particularly active and successful. The sixteenth century in England had a group of scholars, largely antiquarian—Camden, Leland, Hakluyt, and others. The late seventeenth century all over Europe was rich in scholars and scientists. In England there were Newton, Boyle, Cudworth, Bentley, and others. The eighteenth century gave us a great group of Shakespeare scholars culminating in Edmund Malone. Bishop Percy, Thomas Warton, Bishop Hurd, and others were also fair scholars in the English field. Walter Scott was no mean scholar. English scholarship throve actively in the nineteenth century. The Shakespeareans were Halliwell and Collier in the earlier group, Masson, Spedding, Furnivall, and Bullen in the later. Many texts and documents were made available during that period, and the Dictionary of National Biography was well under way before the end of the century. It was then that German scholarship did its greatest work in the English field both in language and literature. Ten Brink, Zupitza, and Sievers were scholars of renown, and there were others. The European scholarly movement was reflected in America in the last quarter of the nineteenth century, and American scholarship in the English field then came to life and became, not only relatively, but actually important. The same impulse passed on into the twentieth century in both England and America, and, however it may have been in literature and the arts, scholarship throve enormously during the interval between the first and second world wars.

The consequence of this long-enduring and great modern period of scholarly activity is that scholarship in English may be said to be in a highly developed state. If one looks at the field from the point of view of major figures and literary forms, one may see everywhere high degrees of development: Beowulf, Chaucer, Shakespeare, Spenser, Milton, Dryden and Pope, Johnson and his contemporaries, Wordsworth and the Romantic school, the novel, the drama, and the essay have all been extensively and effectively studied. American literature is the newcomer in the field, and it has been very greatly and very quickly set in order and interpreted. We now have a dictionary of American biography, an extensive bibliographical apparatus, and a wide publication or republication of texts and documents. One can see also that the period since the first world war has seen great advances in the scholarship dealing with the very greatest figures in the literature, particularly Chaucer, Spenser, Shakespeare, and Milton. Scholarship has been so prosperous and scholars so numerous that the work has been pushed far beyond the major figures and the major subjects and has devoted itself to many minor writers, works, and movements. Photographic reproductions and microfilms have come into common use and have made detailed investigation possible in many places where it could not be carried on before. Publication of scholarly works has tended to lag behind since the great depression, but it too has in general been adequate.

Some interesting questions naturally arise out of the situation which now confronts graduate students in English. Is all the important work already done? Is it possible to devise new points of view and new practices which will give us an even better scholarship?

All the work on the present basis is by no means done. Discovery is still possible in many fields. New manuscripts and hitherto unknown printed books will turn up, new references to old subjects and new facts will be found. Much that has significance has been overlooked, and much error has made its way into literary history and literary criticism and has been repeated in some cases for generations. We are affected on the one side with a paralysis of conservatism and on the other by unrestrained conjecture and speculation. A great job of supplementation and correction seems interesting, imperative, or necessary. In this type of work we require the best possible training and methodology, because it is true that the most easily plucked fruit has usually been gathered. There too is needed superior refinement and discrimination and a wider search in records, in history, and in foreign literature both classical and modern. There is no lack of tasks and the demand is that the tasks shall be better done.

There is another feature also that must not be forgotten. Each age has to study the literature of the past over again for itself in order that it may understand it, apply its teachings, and learn its beauties, because each age has its own proper sense of values and its own ideas of what is true and what constitutes important truth. Each age has therefore the job of re-interpretation. The last generation has rather unexpectedly decided that it will discover the meaning and values of old authors themselves and has pinned its faith to the idea, for example, that Shakespeare's own meaning is the greatest of Shakespearean meanings. It seems to me also that our age has the homely and practical task of combining, integrating, and interpreting the findings of our highly developed research scholarship and carrying them through the minds of our students into the life of our people. I should have little use for literary scholarship if I did not think that its ultimate aim and final result are to make the works of the past more interesting and more significant in life than they were without it. I have a rather high opinion of the improvement of English teaching in America during my professional lifetime, and I attribute at least part of the improvement to the fact that English teachers are in general better scholars than they were a generation or more ago. I do not think we have yet reaped all the profit of a greater command of truth in the teaching of English literature, for there remains a banal ignorance of literary truth in the press and among popular reviewers, an ignorance seemingly ineradicable; but in time, if this war does not throw us too far behind and if we do not lose heart and abandon our standards, we may yet see our nation more enlightened in literary matters than it now is. After all, it is we who have the chance to teach the literary-minded youth and to train the teachers of literature. I think, for example, that satisfactory English prose is far more generally written than it was even a generation ago.

You might be interested also in having me look over the field of English literature and make a few tentative suggestions of areas less well worked and still capable of yielding desirable returns. When I have finished this lecture, I should like to have from you who are present still other suggestions. In the field of Old and Middle English one job great enough to employ a graduate department or several graduate departments for a generation, and demanding also a severe preparation, stands out in my mind with special clarity and attractiveness. I refer to the liturgical basis of almost all mediaeva' literature. I use liturgical in a broad sense to designate all the particularized culture of the mediaeval church. The lack of this knowledge baffles us in the study of Old and Middle English literature in two ways: because we do not know liturgy, we do not know the actual meaning, appreciate the quality, and feel the emotional groundswell of the literature of the period; and because Europe was, culturally speaking, one country during the Middle Ages, intimately inter-related through the Church, we devote ourselves in the study of Old and Middle English literature to one small and often fragmentary section of a great world. I could illustrate this from the difficulties we have had and still have in getting even scholars in the modern world to understand the nature of the religious drama; but I prefer to suggest the issue by the statement of one simple and obvious question: What do you make of the fact that the content of the Junian Manuscript is as a whole and in its parts immediately reflective of the plan of salvation as taught and commemorated in the liturgical year? The manuscript contains accounts of the creation and the fall of man, of the patriarchs, legitimately including, in my judgment, both Moses and Daniel, and then skips over the prophets, the nativity, the ministry and the passion, to begin again with the temptation of our Lord, the resurrection, and the harrowing of hell. Is it not an epical expansion and rendition of the theological idea of Easter as developed also in the earlier Easter plays? Do not think this problem is easy or that it is anything less than typical of almost the whole body of mediaeval literature, of which literature liturgy was the inspiration and morphological force.

I may follow this with the statement that the intense religiosity of the sixteenth and the first half of the seventeenth centuries must have had profound significance in Renaissance literature, although nowhere, except possibly in the case of Milton, determined and realized. I would say also that sixteenth-century education, science, philosophy, and politics, with the popular life and traditions of the age, still offer, although a good deal has been done, opportunities for investigation and interpretation. Elizabethan drama, although widely studied and even implemented, still remains, outside of Shakespeare, Marlowe, Jonson, and a few others, beyond the range of even better literary culture. Seventeenth-century literature, particularly its great body of prose and with it the core of seventeenth-century thought, has not had the attention it deserves. We have not understood, in spite of a body of most illuminating writers, the popular life and culture of the eighteenth century, nor have we realized the greatness of eighteenth-century thought. This is particularly a job for American scholars, for, not only is eighteenth-century literature part and parcel of American literature, but the eighteenth century has great and important things, of which we remain ignorant, to say to the twentieth century. We need to go further in the study of eighteenth-century literature than the growth of English prose style and the forerunners of the Romantic Movement. We need also further, deeper, and truer studies of nineteenth-century literature, with its scientific, philosophic, and social bearings and backgrounds. Dr. Woodrow Wilson used to say, quoting I think Bagehot, that no century ever speaks well of its predecessor, and here we have a well known case in point. We do not fully appreciate the literary greatness of the nineteenth century.

The field of American literature is still comparatively new, but a great deal of excellent scholarly work has already been done in it, and done very quickly. We have, as before said, a dictionary of American biography, and a very good one, and much material threatened with loss has been rescued. I refer not only to the great collections at Harvard, in California, at Ann Arbor and Madison, and in various parts of the South, but to many smaller collections and to extensive publications and republications. It was only this week that I saw various interesting documents in the library of the department of drama in this university, among which was the recently issued series of one hundred American plays. We are now coming to a point where scholars can afford to treat American literature in a less isolated fashion, and can take time to relate it all along the line to English literature and to foreign literatures. We have many patterns of scholarship in the American field which are worth perpetuation, as, for example, a great model from the hand of the late Vernon L. Parrington, patterns which might well be further used in the American field, the English field, or a combination of the two.

Indeed, that statement causes me to make at this time the one suggestion which with my present light I am capable of making. Those of you who have listened to my general lectures will recognize the suggestion as fundamental to that course. I suggest a larger and more comprehensive attack on literary problems, and I recommend for that purpose a broader and more catholic scholarship, with less specialization but with equal or greater intensity. If we adopted such a point of view, we should, I am convinced, acquire the fertility of mind and the courage to undertake individual and joint enterprises of far-reaching and important character. I refer not only to such enterprises as the *Short-Title Catalogue*, the *Cambridge Bibliography of English Literature*, Professor Stith Thompson's index of ballad themes, and the current proposals for the revision and supplementation of Elizabethan biography and the subject-index of early printed books, but to other enterprises in quite unexpected fields. Here again I proceed by suggesting rather vaguely a few problems, and here again I ask for further and better suggestions.

Suppose we as students of fiction and as men of cultivated tastes knew and lamented how repetitious, banal, and essentially improbable are the plots, characters, and significances of most current fiction; suppose us able to resist the pressure of publication clubs, the blurbs of publishers, and the praises of dishonest reviewers, how might we go about the undertaking of creating a better taste in the minds of our pupils and thus disseminating better literary taste in our communities? How could we, with our knowledge of drama and of life and our supposedly better taste, go about the task of discounting the movies for their own good? Certainly not by flattery or by fuzzy thinking. Certainly not by allowing ourselves to be fooled out of our better judgment by technicolor and superficial cleverness into the acceptance of impossible romanticism, immorality, fallacy, sentimentality, and mere convention, even when these things have the endorsement of authority and are made attractive by suggestions of social superiority. How can we make the truth appear in matters of taste? My homely suggestion is that it is only by becoming ourselves embodiments of the qualities we desire to see prevail, for I know of no way of doing the thing except by achieving for ourselves a love of truth, a broad and enlightened recognition of truth, and sufficient firmness of mind to identify its opposite even when that opposite is disguised. How would you go about the task of interesting more college men in American universities in the study of literature? How would you attack the very problem which I have declared is the one in whose solution I think rests the greatest hope, namely, the problem of getting graduate students and their directors to work at once more intensely and on broader lines, so that they might entertain more distant and more aspiring ends? These are all operative problems in the field of culture, but I see no reason why they are beyond our scope, and, if we do not attack them and many others of the kind, I know of no other organized agency which is apt to exert itself. We must remember that in all such beneficent undertakings we can do little at once, but that we have the generations on our side.

With reference to the equipment of the scholar, it will, as I said, depend somewhat on the task to be achieved and on the particular field to be entered. Certainly for language, literature, and composition the preparation is somewhat, although I think not radically, different. I shall speak of it quite in general and of course with the needs of traditional scholarship more closely in mind.

The thing that I should put first is a knowledge of English literature. If circumstances of early education have not made the graduate student in English a reader and a bookman, he enters the profession with a heavy handicap and will have to burn the midnight oil if he wishes to succeed in his own field. The requirement is by no means light, for, not only must the English scholar have covered a vast body of literature as a basal preparation, but he must keep on reading all his life. I have no respect for professors of English and doctors of philosophy who are ignorant of current literature and the course of thought in the modern world. Indeed, I do not see how they can discharge a proper function as interpreters of the past to the present unless they know the present. But I have even less respect for those men trained in the older fields who lack the intellectual muscle to put them over and who take refuge in current literature.

Let me give you gratuitously this counsel: make haste slowly. Do not read too fast and read every book so thoughtfully that you will never need to read it again except for a special purpose or for enjoyment. Much of the older literature, let us say, for example, Elizabethan drama, needs to be read twice or even oftener in order that it may be understood. Wherever possible, when confronted by an original and a commentary or criticism, read the original if it is worth reading—this as a general practice. Reading about books instead of reading the books themselves blurs the impression and no young scholar should suffer himself to develop a vague mind. One way of keeping cobwebs out of the "attic," for example, is to think about Wordsworth, Scott, and Byron, and not about Romanticism; about Shakespeare, Jonson, Congreve, Sheridan, and O'Neill, and not about the technique of the drama or about the usually unworkable classifications of English drama.

Second in importance for the scholar, I think, is the problem of language, and with it I wish to associate composition. It is important that you should know your own language in no casual fashion, and a knowledge of its early forms and also, particularly, of Latin, will help you enter into it. In some fields of operation in English these older forms and Latin itself are simply indispensable. In some areas you may need Old French, Old Norse, or Celtic. You must not only know your own language, but must be able to write and speak it in as great perfection as possible. Here an equally great requirement is laid on scholars in other fields. It may take you a long time to learn to write English well, but do not despair, for better and better style will come to you as you increase in intellectual ability. Language and thought, psychologically speaking, are the obverse and reverse of one and the same medal. I think, if I had a general criticism to make of the English used by scholars, it would be that it is apt to be fragmentary, the thoughts not completely expressed, as, for example, T. H. Huxley expresses them.

Perhaps, as a third element in the equipment of the scholar, I should put Latin and other foreign languages. It has long been recognized that for work in the mediaeval field a knowledge of Latin is mandatory. I should like to repeat this and to add that Latin is the key to some of the greatest opportunities now open to Renaissance scholars. Europe during the Renaissance was still pretty much one and the same in its culture, and Latin was still the medium of exchange. Renaissance culture was, moreover, a derivative from the culture of the ancient world, particularly of ancient Rome, and this aspect of the matter tends to make Latin a necessary part of the Renaissance scholar's equipment. In any case, Latin for Renaissance workers is to be regarded as a means of unlocking opportunity. Add to this, that records and legal documents of every sort were still largely written in Latin, and its importance becomes still more obvious. I should like to present the case of other foreign languages as means of broadening the scholar's scope and strengthening his hand. French, Italian, and to a less degree Spanish are, to say the very least, valuable accomplishments well nigh indispensable, and German, because of the importance of German scholarship, has become so. The literary world has been and still is pretty closely united, and the scholar soon passes beyond the area in which the works he needs to read have been translated into his own tongue, so that one would say that English scholars will most of them find it highly advantageous to know foreign languages as well as foreign literatures. Greek stands by itself. It may be neglected as lacking in utility, but its need is personal, like the grace of God.

In the fourth place, let me for a special reason make a special heading of paleography and diplomatics. It is now possible for large numbers of relatively isolated scholars to procure at quite moderate costs the use of manuscript material in practically every field in which it is available anywhere. The great collections of Britain, France, and Italy, which I hope the ravages of war have spared, are unbelievably rich, and the workers are limited in numbers, interest, and ability. Reproductions are easy to procure. Much of the work that has been done on manuscripts needs to be done over again, and there is a great forest, a vast area, as yet untouched. Scholars in all the older fields need to know paleography, and paleography is an art which can be studied at home as well as abroad. A practical part of this subject for us who are students of English and for students in various historical fields is a knowledge of social, religious, and governmental organization in use in the Middle Ages and the Renaissance. The modern student needs to know what records were made for what purposes by what officials—by the officers of parishes, dioceses, and eccleasiastical courts, by coroners, justices of the peace, and the clerks of various courts, by legislative assemblies, and by the sovereign's government itself. The scholar needs to know the procedure governing the making˙ of records, and the channels through which official business passed. Such information is not easy to get. Discoveries by many older scholars and some quite recent ones show how important such knowledge may be.

Closely connected with a knowledge of records is a knowledge of history, and no vague, general knowledge will do. The knowledge needs to descend to individuals, families, groups, political parties, and economic and religious interests. Records are not about causes and policies; they are about people and events. Historians are taught how to use documents and how to determine truth from them. Students of the history of literature need to know the historical method and to be trained in it. They need it as badly as the historians themselves.

From the many other possible needs in the equipment of the scholar I shall select two. I mention first philosophy both in its general tenets and influences and in its particular manifestations. A scholar is relatively helpless who does not know the doctrines of Plato and Aristotle and does not understand, for example, the significance of the shift from Aristotelianism to Stoicism and materialism at the end of the Renaissance. Secondly, I mention religion and its history. I do this on general as well as special grounds. Religion was during by far the longest period of English culture—the Middle Ages, the Renaissance, and for a long time after the waning of the Renaissance—the custodian of knowledge and culture. It was moreover the subject of greatest warmth. Its quarrels were world quarrels, and its differences were the dividing lines between men and nations. Religion was surely a motive force of the great writers of the early periods and of many great writers since.

I shall close this lecture with a caution and a consolation. You yourselves are where you are of your own volition. Therefore, get the idea out of your heads, if you have it there, that the world owes you anything in favor of the idea that you owe the world more than you can ever pay. You may remember that the Second Citizen objects to doing anything for Coriolanus on the ground that Coriolanus "pays himself with being proud" (*Cor.* I, i, 33-4). Every scholar knows in his heart that he would not exchange the freedom of his mind and the power of his position for the richest sinecure in the gift of the richest American corporation and looks down with sure disdain on the so-called applied scientist who sells his brains to industry. He knows that unrewarded effort sustains character and that truth yields herself only to an unselfish quest. The true scholar snaps his fingers at the foundations and does his stuff whether he gets a "grant" or not. Such a position is the most enviable I know of in all the world and is rivaled only by that of divines and philanthropists. The temper of the time is no doubt against scholarship; it has been so in some measure always. Perhaps it is now more obnoxiously vocal than ever; but it does not matter, for we are the people whose business it is to find out what is the matter with those fellows who despise us. Even the difficulty of the job lends zest to it. Humanity has a serious objection to being improved; and, remember, we seek to improve it. Bacon puts it this way: "*Hercules, when he went to unbind Prometheus* (by whom human nature is represented), *sailed the length of the great ocean in an earthen pot or pitcher.*" Particularly, I ask you to join with me in the scorn of those quacks who are so fond of telling us that these hard things are easy.

I am now an older scholar. The pressures and necessities of personal interest have long ago ceased to have any weight with me, and the time left for achievement has grown I know not how short. In these circumstances I grow anxious that the ideas I have formed about the scholar's work and the scholar's life should be passed on as generously as possible to others who are following or may intend to follow the long and arduous, albeit eminently satisfactory, road which I have traveled.

CHAPTER X

COLLEGES AND UNIVERSITIES
IN A POST-WAR WORLD*

Duty and interest are perfectly coincident; for the most part in this world, but entirely and in every instance if we take in the future, and the whole; this being in the notion of a good and perfect administration of things. Thus they who have been so wise in their generation as to regard only their own supposed interest, at the expense and to the injury of others, shall at last find, that he who has given up all the advantages of the present world, rather than violate his conscience and the relations of life, has infinitely better provided for himself, and secured his own interest and happiness.

I CONFESS some embarrassment in coming before you to lecture on so hackneyed a subject as "Colleges and Universities in a Post-War World." I can only justify myself on two grounds: I am actually a pioneer in the field, since on February 2, 1943, I addressed on this subject the Faculty Luncheon Club of the University of North Carolina (See *Bull.*, Amer. Assn. Univ. Professors, Vol. XXIX, No. 2.) The great flood of books and articles on the universities in the post-war world is, as far as I know, subsequent to that not very remote date. I may also say that, so far as I can see, no great attention has been paid to what I said, and what seem to me the best things I said have not been repeated by anybody else. Here then, to begin with, are some excerpts from my former paper:

By and by the soldiers will come back. I believe this because I once saw them come back, indeed, came back with them. Our students will return to the universities probably pretty much as they did before. They came back then in large numbers, and for four or five years our classes were full of men who had been under arms. But the students who returned were not entirely the same students who went away, and those who return to us will not be exactly the same students who have recently left us. Instead of boys they will be young men who have had experience with actual affairs. I shall never forget the interest I felt in teaching them after the first world war. They were not cleverer than other younger students, but they had a gratifying appreciation of actual

---

*Lecture before the faculty of the University of Washington.

values. They knew when things were valid and not mere entertainment and idle talk. We may expect a similar attitude on their part when they return again. It is a mistake to think they will have much to teach us, but they will certainly insist on our teaching them a great deal and, in general, things of actual value.

We have now a lull in the university world in the midst of this disturbance. Our students are fewer and the mill is grinding less grist. We might and, I think, should use this interim for the purpose of taking stock, or determining our course, or getting our house in order, or any way you wish to phrase it. It would be a pity, as it was twenty years ago, and something of a disgrace to us not to be able to offer those soldiers, sailors, and aviators something of real value, something that will command their respect, something they would be willing to use as guidance in life and able to use as a means of their re-establishment in civil society.

The problem in American universities has been, not so much how to train and instruct students, as how to get them to study, how to secure and hold their attention in the midst of countless diversions, many quackeries, and a disposition on their own part toward idleness. The intellectual life of our student bodies has been, I think most of us would admit, on a low level.

There are two general courses of procedure. The first is a description of the remedies we have tried to apply during recent years, and the second is an old principle which has been forgotten, or nearly so. I shall state them both.

1. Improve our methodology. Do more careful and skillful teaching. Plan courses of study more scientifically. Get acquainted with students. Hold many conferences. Introduce tutorial methods into our instruction. Devise ways by which students may express themselves. 2. Let members of university faculties devote themselves to research, productive scholarship, so as to gain and maintain intellectual leadership in their respective fields.

I offer diffidently the following criticisms of plan one. Expert teaching is desirable, but not so necessary in dealing with mature men and women, as is something which will induce students voluntarily to apply their powers in the pursuit of a knowledge they wish really to possess. Of course students should be treated well. Our present attitude toward them is by and large extremely cordial. The great intellectual leaders I have known in the university world always knew their students. There may be some who do not, but it does not greatly matter, provided they are leaders. . The proper treatment of students may be taken for granted along with good manners, a clean and properly dressed person, and the ability to speak in such a way as can be understood. It is possible that in some institutions we have gone too far in the matter of advising students, holding conferences with them, and mothering them, and have wasted a good deal of time which might better have been spent in study on their part and on ours. As for teaching modern students to express themselves, it is a much over-rated device. Our modern students are not as a class bashful. Certainly they are not so in the West. If any of them are found on observation to need encouragement, they should by all means receive it. When a student has something to say, and it is our business to see to it that he acquires something to say, let us by all means give him a chance to say it. Let us go further and provide him with practical advice on the handling of his material and his manner of delivery. This is a different thing from the turning of our classrooms into bicker sessions. Let me quote an interesting and pertinent passage from *Essays and Sketches* (Yale University Press) by the late Kemper Fullerton:

In Berlin I came under the influence of one of the greatest scholars and teachers of the nineteenth century, Adolph Harnack. From him I unconsciously imbibed something of the hard, cold, scientific spirit which I had deprecated in college because it was associated in my mind with mathematics, and challenged in the seminary because it was associated with the German criticism of the Bible. But now it was neither hard nor cold but glowing with the imaginative insight and enthusiasm of a really great personality. How glad I am that the discussion-group method had not yet supplanted the lecture system of those days, and that I had the chance to feel the power and mastery of Harnack rather than to have my own ignorance enlarged by the ignorance of my fellow students.

This quotation is not of course presented as an argument for the lecture system as against the inductive method ordinarily used in seminars. It is cited mainly as an illustration of the influence of a great scholar in the university pursuing whatever method he chooses to pursue.

We have probably not been able to establish as completely as we should what is referred to as the "professional attitude." Some universities in spite of difficulties breed and maintain that attitude. I have reason to think that it still exists in some institutions. It was very strong at Chicago in my day. I found it in the German universities years ago and at Oxford. I do not think we have enough of it in American universities. Indeed, an earnest, sincere, businesslike attitude toward their work on the part of students is too rare, and yet it is the feature of our work that counts most.

Is it not true that this professional attitude on the part of the student is the immediate result of such an attitude on the part of the university teacher? If the university teacher knows his stuff, if he believes in it enough to work at it (instead, let us say, of working at direct social betterment), will not his students, because of his example, his earnestness and his achievements, also believe in the subject enough to work at it? The answer is that students have always done so and always will do so. If this is true of the individual teacher, is it not true of the institution as a whole? The result of a widely current set of such attitudes we might describe as an atmosphere. Students and teachers alike will be industrious in their studies and we shall have an intellectual atmosphere.

This principle seems to be illustrated in the histories of great universities and in the histories of universities not now great which have had periods or episodes of greatness. Many universities in our country have acquired the necessary equipment for greatness. They have buildings, libraries, laboratories, faculties made up of doctors of philosophy, and everything needed except industry and perseverance. They are often ready to go, but cannot start their wheels. A pressure from the community is brought to bear on them and they resort to the projects of specialists. They institute all sorts of devices pertaining to moral suasion—educational methodology, student guidance, social improvement, what not. Whereas they need to have their faculties go to work as "faculties."

This may not be a panacea, but there is so much evidence to support it that it seems to be one, and why should it not be? The intellectual leadership of society, the progress of the arts and sciences, the correct transmission and interpretation of the *traditio*, the invigoration of the mind of the age—these things, or rather this thing, is the function of the university. If we do not believe in our vocation enough to work at it, we are either unfaithful servants or persons wandering in the forest who have lost the true and only way. The tragedy of it is that in our moral solicitude we spend hours in interviews and conferences which ought to be spent in study and thought, in scholarship and research. It must be said to the discredit of our present system that it has probably spoiled a great many of our younger men. They have not only been overloaded with teaching, but have been so involved in methods and regulations that they have no time to study. They have had also too little encouragement to do so. The shrewder ones have realized that social and not scholarly activity is the road to promotion, and, since social activity is much easier than the labor of learning and the work of creation, they have grown ignorant and lazy. The point is of course that they would make much better teachers if they were making progress in the mastery of their subjects.

It is necessary and becoming that in a case of this kind we should be reasonable and practical. We should, for example, inquire what we mean by scholarship and research. After the hasty American fashion these words have been narrowed, if not distorted, in their meanings. Research has come to mean discovery of new knowledge; whereas research is properly an individual matter. It is the exercise of an inquiring mind, and the principle of research applies as truly to a college freshman as it does to a doctor of laws. There is a big element of luck in all discovery, and we cannot compel men to have good luck. The field has also a great deal to do with it. In the older well-worked disciplines discovery is not easy. Each situation also controls the possibilities of making actual contributions to the sum of the world's knowledge. In certain places and situations the thing may be well-nigh impossible of achievement, but the power of the individual scholar to know his subject and to make his unique contribution to the interpretation of that subject is nowhere limited, nor is the possibility of keeping abreast of the advancement of his subject in any way hampered.

Then again we have made an absurd union between scholarship or research and publication. These things have no necessary relation to each other, and the marriage is so obnoxious to the minds of all reasonable university men that scholarship and publication should be divorced. It is true that it is useful to have work published and rendered available to other scholars. It is also true that we university teachers usually belong by nature to the expressive type of humanity and that certain of us are made happy by seeing our names in print. But not all of us. Let no man of intellectual integrity be clubbed over the head by the crude notion (or even requirement) that he must publish such and such a number of articles or lose his standing. University teachers should have the freedom to work at something of deep as well as of current importance, and, if they do not get their books finished before they die, it is just too bad; but meantime, while they have worked and thought, they have been scholars in society and beacons of light in the generation.

Scholarship has also come to mean something dry or something so trivial or so highly specialized as to be unintelligible or insignificant. When these charges are true, and they are not true nearly so often as they are said to be, it is the fault of the scholar and not of scholarship. Unless scholarship as a whole makes life better, more intelligible, and even more interesting, it is not worth fooling with. But it does as an occupation do just these things. Fortunately life is a very varied thing, and interests are very catholic. One should not dogmatize on the subject of what is interesting or important. There is a certain wholesome glow and touching human sympathy in the old story of the philologist who in his lectures had approached a climax and a great new division of his subject. He began his lecture with the words, "Gentlemen, the Dative!"

There is one other popular misinterpretation of our proper activities. The scientists, for example, have been much pestered by those who think that research in science should always be directed toward something of a practical and remunerative nature. This idea is so puny and contemptible that we may pass it over without remark.

By way of summary I should say that for practical purposes a scholar may be described as one who has an adequate and persevering mastery of his subject.

Our interests on this occasion are really in what our universities are going to be after the war. We have, some of us, a period of relative leisure in which to make up our minds about what we mean to do. The surest and most honorable plan is to begin now to work very hard at our subjects. I believe that, if we do this, the result will be that we shall be of great use to our soldier students when they return to us. They will want the very truth of the matter about, let us say, chemistry, history, and political science. Some of them may wish to work out careers in the field of the interpretation of literature. They will wish to find men who are masters of these subjects and an atmosphere in our universities which is seriously intellectual. Let us therefore work at our subjects and not waste our time in trying to prepare beforehand for unknown and unpredictable events or in vain attempts to adjust social relationships. I believe also that any institution which follows this policy will make itself great among the universities of our country.

On the basis of a philosophy of higher education to which I adhere very strongly I have tried to describe a policy which has historical validity as well as immediate utility. What I have recommended is not a reaction but a restoration and revival. I hope that we shall retain all of the merits of recent discovery in educational methodology and use them in the discharge of our proper and original function in civilized society. I have had no particular university in mind while I spoke and no particular university teacher in mind except myself.

There are some matters immediately or remotely connected with the post-war world about which I am uncertain, but which have nevertheless sufficient importance to make me wish to bring them before you. War is a great breeder of fear, and, strangely enough, that fear is not manifested, perhaps not really felt, until the war is over. While the war is on, we brace ourselves to face the situation, and show, not only fortitude, but actual daring; but when the war is over, we find ourselves trembling and apprehensive. After the first world war our country was beset with a great, unreasonable, conservative reaction. It may be so again, and it behooves us to anticipate it. Because of this fearful conservatism selfish interests and unscrupulous people took advantage of our timidity, and even universities failed to recognize, accept, and adapt themselves to change. Perhaps we suspected all change as inimical and shut our eyes to every altered aspect. In other words, we failed to discriminate between conditions that were definitely altered and conditions which only seemed so. Great liberal programs worthy of the educational institutions of a great republic were laid aside. We wrote "Safety First," not as our motto, but as our creed. We returned to the politics of a generation before, that time when we were permitting our so-called loyal leaders to filch from us the public domain and seize our natural resources into their own private hands. We were so afraid of interfering with business that we sat and let ourselves be robbed. It seemed as if the prophecy was being fulfilled: "God hath chosen the foolish things of the world to confound the wise; and God hath chosen the weak things of the world to confound the mighty."

Now it is certain that no man knows what the issues of the

post-war world will be; but I think we may fairly anticipate that a national conservative reaction will arise out of our natural fear. I have made it clear that I dread nothing so much as a conservative return to the sort of university world we have had in the inter- bellum period. I have said that I should like to see the faculties of universities reassert and regain their control over higher educa- tion, and my counsel to that end is contained in the text, "Be not overcome of evil, but overcome evil with good."

If I am wrong about some of the things which I think ought to be done, I should like to know it, for I think they are matters of importance which should receive wise attention and considered and persevering action. If I am wrong, there is of course nothing to be done.

I think that very widely in American institutions of higher learning the faculties have lost control of those institutions as institutions and that the situation is in the long run fraught with danger. Men of learning should control higher education and historically have always done so. I do not know of any other social group who have at once the ability, the knowledge, and the personal interest to do the job. One of the reasons for this loss of authority in our own house is the intense power and the extent of the social rivalries which now confront us. Our competitor has been the modern world with its automobiles and their power to minimize distance, the movies, the radio, the development of enter- tainment as a business, into which has gone capital by the billion, and, finally, a spread of luxury with its highly organized social pleasures. One might add the breakdown of the authority of the American home, which has itself been the victim of these same dif- fusive and mainly inimical forces. At any rate, it seems to me that these various things, or some of them at least, have so affected homes, schools, and high schools that students in dangerous numbers come to us already spoiled, headstrong, and filled with false ideals. Many of them have come to the university, not for anything we have to offer them, but for athletics, social advantage, social life, and a good time. The press, reflecting an unenlightened public opinion, backs them up, discipline is very difficult, and even the right and necessity of it is in dispute and is in many places in- effective, so that I think I may hazard the statement that we are no longer running our own show. It might at least be granted that we are not doing a good job of it. The control of the public behavior of the student body has usually been turned over to special administrative authorities, and this seems to be wise and practical; but I think we have no right to wash our hands of the matter and to assume an attitude of indifference as to the kind of lives our students lead in universities. Historically the control is, or should be, our responsibility, and I do not think it safe or even self-respecting to let it slide. If it were only a matter of letting the devil claim his own, there might be something to be said for it; but we must realize that there is still in this country a very large majority of simple, honest citizens, and that it is our duty to provide for their children an environment of health and not corruption. During my academic life I have met, as you have, many parents, and I have found that they desire, first of all, that they should have good and industrious children, that their primary desire for their children is, not that they should excel in athletics and social activity, or even that they should learn to be smart about money-making, but that their children should be in the way of becoming what we call good citizens. I think that a great deal of the selfish materialism in our student body is campus-bred, and I have wondered if we are really in our actual, effective performance as good as the people we serve. Idle and diverted students not only contribute nothing to our educational effort, but they divert or corrupt many others who come with good intentions and with the potentiality of making a good use of the best we are able to offer. I think also that these hordes of inattentive students are breaking down to some extent our own faith in education and injuring the morale of many of our younger faculty men.

As far as I can see we are, however unwilling we may be to admit it, relatively helpless in the matter of controlling the moral features of the lives of our students. We may through our faculty assemblies regain directive, legislative control of student discipline, but, in the meantime, I think our position is one of weakness. We are therefore thrown back to our last line of defense, which I believe to be ultimately effective and capable of withstanding the attack. I refer to academic standards. This field is organic, and in it we are not and need never be in a hopeless position. We have the knowledge and ability to uphold academic standards if we are only able and willing to exercise them. Our duty as public servants, our professional honor, and our self-respect as scholars call upon us to see to it that our work be done and our degrees earned. But the matter is not easily achieved, and in my judgment we are failing and falling back. There are weak spots in our lines through which the enemy infiltrates our position and we suffer continual defeat. Those loopholes are mainly snap-courses and ill-organized, inefficient, and sometimes unscrupulous departments. The thing usually happens because teachers and departments desire to gain the prestige and advantage of large numbers or fanatically believe that they are entitled to crowd other teachers and departments out of the race. Other teachers and departments which would not otherwise do so lower their requirements in order to protect themselves, so that it has come about that almost everywhere our standards are too low. Our students spend three-fourths of their time playing or courting or loafing, as if we were not factors in their lives at all. There is no business or profession in which learners have as little to do as they have in ours. Our effective requirements are simply trivial. It is not unusual to see industrious students of average ability work eight hours out of every twenty-four for their livings and yet satisfy in the most abundant way all of our requirements for degrees.

If I am even approximately near the truth in what I have said, something ought to be done about this situation. I can think of nothing so obvious to do, as a first step, as for faculties to urge upon administrators that they patch up the holes in our lines and make an effort to secure for us a united front by organizing our academic public opinion for our protection. We can withhold credits and degrees from the unworthy and we know how to do it, and we can by the determined and persevering use of these means, I believe, build up a more studious undergraduate body. We can thus go a long way toward reassuming our mastery of our own house. Let us be frank about this matter. Dances are really and actually more fun than examinations. Movie stars are much more attractive to the young than are any college professors, and I think college professors might as well admit the fact. There is more pleasurable notoriety in winning an athletic contest, joining a fashionable fraternity or sorority, or being chosen to high undergraduate offices than there is in receiving A's in college classes. We might as well recognize this situation, and I do not see how any frank person can fail to do so. The young people of this age may, so far as I am concerned, lead as furious social lives as they please. Perhaps they are entitled to do so and, in any case, will probably do so irrespective of my wishes. But I see no reason why the academic profession should allow them to scuff American higher education un⌐   ⌐ soles of their dancing feet.

I have emphasized my belief that by and large the academic profession in America is made up of men who know their jobs and are, as a group of men, not only intelligent and industrious, but conscientious. I see no reason why they should be thwarted, and I believe that, if they put their minds and wills to work, they can win. If we win a victory over the rather ill-organized social forces which now imperil us, we shall not only improve our professional situation, but shall accomplish the greatest thing for our country that could possibly be accomplished. I would not exaggerate the difficulties. The academician has been at war with the barbarian for thousands of years. We know what to do and how to do it, and there is no mystery about it. My job is to attend to the training of workers in the field of literature, yours to produce chemists, historians, mathematicians, economists, and what not. I think we know how to do these jobs. I heard Woodrow Wilson once say in a faculty meeting, "I know better what any sophomore ought to study than that sophomore himself knows," and I think he was right. There are a lot of reformers who have been telling us that everything we have been doing is wrong. I admire their zeal and their courage, and I am willing to give them a hearing, but I think they are wrong in being too inclusive and too uncritical. No doubt some of the things we have been doing are erroneous and need to be set right. I do not think the criticism applies to the job as a whole. I do not believe I am altogether mistaken about this business of teaching English literature. If I am, it is a case of stupidity and not inattention. I too have been alive and have been an earnest, thinking, industrious man all my life, and I am not willing to admit that I do not know what I have been doing for more than forty years. I would not, however, rest the case on my own merits, but I would rest it on the merits that I believe you have, you and many thousands of college and university teachers in America. We all know that we do not so much need to find new things to do and new ways of doing them as to do old things well.

There is no essential difference between the training needed by good citizens in time of peace and in time of war. The training needs to be good in both cases. Even emergency educational service for war is, by and large, nothing except an additional effort to do more quickly what we are supposed to do anyhow. In so far as it is poorly done it is to that degree not worth doing. There is no economy in lowering standards. A man either knows a thing or possesses a skill or he does not. On this point let me again quote my colleague Professor E. W. Knight of the University of North Carolina ("Education in War and Peace," *North Carolina Education*, Jan., 1943):

> It is, of course, a responsibility of education in this emergency to do everything possible and intelligent to help in winning the war. Another responsibility, however, is to try to do better what [education] is supposed to do anyway, and to be vigilant in preserving and maintaining as creditable standards as possible. It must resist the temptation to be cheap.

Cheapness defeats itself, and I think Professor Knight would agree with me in saying that the doctrine has been needed in American education before the war, is needed during the war, and will be needed after the war is over.

Even if we felt sure *a priori* that our salvation lay in a greater socialization of our universities and in a complete change in educational techniques, we have back of us enough unsuccessful experience to make us question, if not abandon, these ideas. I may be wrong, and yet I must honestly say that in my observation and experience the intellectual interests of our students have been growing fewer during the last quarter of a century. I do not speak of their characters, dispositions, or personal refinement, but confine my statement to their intellectual interests. If these interests have not been diminishing, at least we can say that they have not, as a whole, increased as much as we hoped they would. Back of this paper lies the assumption that after a reasonable number of months or years this war, like the last one, will come to an end. If great disaster overwhelms our nation, conditions may be very different from those presupposed. I think, however, the principles discussed are valid, and in the present situation I know of nothing so important to suggest as that we do now, without tarrying for any reason, go to work at our jobs, jobs which we know perfectly well how to do. I think also that the anticipated future situation will be, not only an emergency, but, if we take advantage of it, a great opportunity for the re-establishment of the highest education on a sound basis. I continue my discussion of some of the not too serious things which stand in our way.

Some writers on education in the post-war world are saying that trustees and administrators have robbed faculties of their liberty, that universities are governed by autocratic power, and that the university ought to be exemplary in its application of democratic principles. No informed, thoughtful person would deny that freedom is necessary to higher education. There are no doubt colleges and universities in the country which are governed autocratically, and I for one think it a very bad thing. I think, however, that in most places our administrative officers are still ultimately responsible to us, since we are necessary to their success. In my own experience I have found them extremely anxious to have the cooperation and support of faculties. Most of them have been men wise enough to know that a considered general enactment works better than an individual enactment, and the faculty has usually been called upon to participate fully in university government. It is too bad when an administrator is a timid soul and afraid to debate his ideas with other men or when he lacks faith in the judgment of a responsible and enlightened majority. I do not think that many administrators would oppose such raising of standards as I have advocated.

I should like in connection with standards to speak of certain newer disciplines. Candor compels me to say at the outset that I think they are coming on well and that they are not often offenders against standards. Because of my own well known sympathetic cooperation with the new department which devotes itself to acting drama and the operation and management of the theater, I select it. I feel an additional assurance that I shall not give offense because of the brilliant success achieved by your own School of Drama at the University of Washington. If any institution of higher learning establishes such a department, it should not be a bed of ease for idle students, and it will not be if the men in charge of it demand excellence, not mere endeavor and manipulative skill, in the mastery of one of the most difficult, the most varied, and the most deeply cultural of human arts. If we have plays without literary or artistic value, ill understood, in which the actors speak with utter unintelligibility and in which costuming, makeup, and histrionic technique are imitative, not of life, but of the comic strip, we are wasting our students' time and blasting their cultural opportunity. To equate such an exercise with the work of mathematicians, sober scientists, and cultivated historians and literary men is absurd. When society demands of the universities new disciplines and types of training, by all means let them be installed and let them assume their share of general academic responsibility. Let education, sociology, commerce, journalism, and others take their places in the line and hold the sectors they are supposed to hold. Let them not give way before the dangerous and insidious attacks of popular demand and let them not be disconcerted by their as yet poorly organized corpus of instruction, for they can always demand and secure individual excellence in their pupils.

I have something I hope not too vague to say about the qualitative aspect of academic life. It is a subject to which attention is rarely directed. I might say that I am going to talk to you about being too busy. It is a mistake to think that the diffusive modern world is affecting our students and passing us by. We too are its victims. It is robbing us of the power and habit of thought, in some cases perhaps of the ability to think. Thought is a well understood process, said to be an operation in which, to quote James, "an extracted character is taken as equivalent to the entire datum from which it comes; and, second, the character thus taken suggests a certain consequence more obviously than it was suggested by the total datum as it originally came." Genius is said to rest on association by similarity, and, although thought has the speed of lightning, it takes time, and paradoxically enough, it also saves time. We are often too busy to think and therefore cannot get our work done. When you have so much to do that you cannot possibly get it done in the time at your disposal, I seriously suggest that, in order that you may finish your task on time, you play a game of golf or take a turn in the victory garden. It works for me and has worked for many years. I could never have turned out the large quantities of alas! mediocre work that I have turned out if I had suffered myself to be rushed off my feet by a lot of business, really unimportant or quickly disposed of, or if I had ever had the habit of working long hours.

Our profession is a profession, not only of action, but of thought. We have difficult things to do and many of them. Our only salvation lies in discrimination between things that are more important and things that are less important. The tempo of our society is rapid. It affects us in many ways. We tend, for example, to work too long hours in order to satisfy our tender consciences and gain a reputation for zeal. We are seduced by the ideal of flying about from place to place and of seeming to be important, rather than productive and effective. The consequence is that we waste our energies and get too little done that amounts to anything. We lack time to think, and we get out of the habit of thinking. Even our references and specialties grow dim in our minds. We might do fewer things and do them so well that they will not have to be done over again, which is another way of suggesting that we spend far more time in thought.

Blunders of this kind have a way of exacting a penalty, and it may be (I am very doubtful about it) that we are threatened with a very serious penalty in this connection. It may be that the hurry and diffusion of our lives are serving to diminish both the quantity and importance of research and productivity in many American universities. It is not enough that we should have graduate students doing research as a part of their training. It is most necessary that the mature scholars in university faculties should continue their weightier productivity. The business of investigation will go on irrespective of what the universities do. Independent research institutes in considerable numbers are already being founded and are attracting and absorbing creative forces. It will not help them very greatly for universities, except certain wealthy eastern institutions, to fall out of the race, it will be a bad thing for the country as a whole, and worst of all for the institutions which become permanently dealers in secondary knowledge and applied science. Dr. Henry E. Sigerist ("The University's Dilemma," *Bull. Hist. Medicine*, June, 1943, pp. 1-13) puts it this way:

> University education becomes sterile the moment it is divorced from research. History has demonstrated this over and over again. What makes higher education is just the fact that young people are granted the privilege to spend a number of years at the source of learning in close touch with men whose life-work is devoted to the advancement of knowledge. . . . The professor becomes older every year, but his students remain eternally young . . . . this contact with a constantly rejuvenating mankind is a great stimulus to him. It makes him look beyond the boundary of his generation, and he who is in research is working for the future, [and], with and through his students, can help in shaping tomorrow's world.

I think enough time and energy, now diffused, could be saved to do all of our local duties well and at the same time double our productivity. There may be nothing in this, but I rather think it is worth more than a passing thought. It is not likely that we, any more than our pupils, shall get any more out of our academic lives than we put into them.